THE CHINESE PRIORITY

by

Rory Carrick

Contents

The chinese priority   1

China's Challenge   7

The Chinese management GAP   11
  I – Creativity   11
  II - The Chinese Priority   15
  III - Retention   19
    i Marriage   20
    ii Education   21
    iii Keeping up with the Joneses   25
    iv Allegiance   34
  IV - Imagination   37
  V - Organizational development   38
  VI – Motivation   40
  VII – Summary   51

What *do* we have to work with? — 53

   I - Eagerness to Learn. — 54

      i. Continuous learning — 56

      ii The ability to learn — 57

      iii Operations — 58

   II - Teamwork — 59

   III - Positive attitude — 60

   IV - Executers — 62

   V - The power of the relationship — 68

      i. The weakness of the contract — 69

      ii Dealing with a dispute — 71

      iii Building the relationship — 75

   Summary: What we have to work with — 82

Taking on the Management gap challenge — 83

   I - Understanding the motivators — 85

   II - Communicating the Vision — 86

   III - Solving the retention problem — 87

      i. On-Boarding — 90

      i Career Plan — 92

      iii Training — 96

      iv Compensations & Benefits — 98

      v Working Environment — 100

vi Work life balance	101
IV - Solving the Creativity Gap	104
V - Developing leaders	107
VI Ensuring Development & Growth	125

Closing 128

CHINA'S CHALLENGE

The fact that China has become an economic giant is no secret anymore, but the West still holds the advantage, for the moment. Many factors will come into play to determine if China will really eclipse the U.S. and Europe in terms of sheer muscle and Japan in terms of absolute quality. We could argue that the untapped domestic demand from within China alone is enough to keep driving this present growth right to the point where the U.S. becomes a net exporter to supply the Chinese demand. We might even talk about the RMB replacing the USD as the global currency.

Even if these conjectures come to fruition, what does that really prove? It proves that the Chinese have the ability to bring their 1.3 billion people out of the Dark

Ages and into the modern world, where everyone has a washing machine and a motor car. Through pure magnitude of the population, China has the ability to look like the superpower of the world. However, this may look impressive from the outside, but it is really only the low-hanging fruit that China is able to reach. China can operate within its own walls in a controlled way that ensures domestic growth, but this is not very impressive. What would be impressive is if it could really conquer the world economy.

China's full potential, or entitlement if you like, is what the U.S. has already achieved, but China's full potential is threefold. China has the ability to be the country that moves up the food chain and brings Africa into prosperity as it has to gear up its manufacturing sector to provide for the Chinese demand. China has the ability to be the leader in R&D and market leaders in high-end luxury products. This would force the U.S. and Europe to accept their station of being the turnkey provider for designs and ideas coming out of the East. China's true potential can be met when you simply take a look at what they have achieved over the last 30 years in education alone. Then extend that to the other 60% of the population in the western parts of China that haven't been exposed to this yet. Unfortunately for China and fortunately for the U.S., there is a significant gap that needs to be overcome in the mindset of the average Chinese before the country's full potential can be realized. This is deeply cultural and will hold them back from ever achieving anything further than domestic growth and modernization. They will never be accepted on the global playing field unless they learn to adapt and play by the rules already defined by the West.

The secret to outperforming the U.S. and reaching their true potential is not in their cheap labor or huge workforce. It is in their management and in the leaders of their corporations. Global companies have invested in China and sent over their Western leaders to manage these businesses. They have done this because they are unable to find local leaders to manage their subsidiaries in a way that allows them to compete as global companies. Hiring local executives would result in the subsidiaries being fully Chinese and ultimately operating independently of the rest of the company and its culture. They have found that local talent cannot represent their company on a global level. If China ever wants to expand their local companies into the global arena, they will need to close some significant gaps in their management and leadership ability.

Firstly, I will try to define the challenges that the current managers have ahead of them before they will be admitted onto the world stage. These challenges are referred to as the Chinese Management Gap.

Section Two will focus on the extensive positive attributes that are lacking in the West but that we see in the Chinese work style and in their culture. This is defined as the Chinese Advantage.
Section Three discusses practical ways to use the Chinese Advantage to overcome the Gap to prepare the Chinese for the global playing field.

Note that these ideas and solutions are not based on vast surveys or studies into the Chinese sociology or psychology. If you are looking for a book that has academic merit built off theories from a classroom, then this is not the book for you. What I offer is a practical guide based on my experience over the last twenty-four years while working in South Africa, in the United States, Singapore, and in China. Although I have found the corporate and company culture differences interesting between South Africa and the U.S., it was Asia, and in particular China, that really offered a challenge for me to understand and improve as I worked with these wonderful people.

If you are an American and reading this, you are probably starting from a media-biased opinion of the Chinese. Read on, and you will have a glimpse of the real China office worker, where you will see that they have similar challenges and strengths, but they also have some significantly pronounced advantages over your teams that should worry you a little and hopefully inspire you to improve your own U.S. teams.

If you are Chinese or Asian and reading this book, you should be proud of the values I highlight, but I fear that I have insulted you in the way I have characterized the gaps your culture has afforded you. So please bear in mind that there is absolutely nothing wrong with the way you do things in China, as long as they are done in China. This book is about showing you the way to compete outside of your borders on a playing field where the West has already defined the rules of the game and the way it is played.

THE CHINESE MANAGEMENT GAP

I – Creativity

The Chinese are typically thought of as copiers. They will take apart a superior Western product, reverse engineer it, and produce an inferior product to sell in the local Chinese market. Usually it will look the same, smell the same, but not operate the same. A similar sounding name and logo will be developed to cause an association in the brain with the original brand, and it will be marketed within China. The Chinese are not known for their original thinking. They find it easier to follow and copy.

Now imagine a 5th grade school classroom. In the West, teachers are trying to encourage individualism and creativity. In China, we are sitting in a classroom with 50 other students, leaning over our desk, while writing and rewriting Chinese characters to enhance the memory and master the art. Multiplication tables, long passages, and poems are committed to memory and then tested. A huge capacity for memorization is developed, leaving no room for creativity.

Conformity has been encouraged historically and has continued in the modern-day classroom, although it is more relaxed in public life. A strong culture of conformity drives home a clear message that standing out from your peers is not acceptable. Excellence in testing is demanded, and the testing is very memory based, focusing on Math and Chinese, both taught though repetition and memorizing.

This general classroom culture of conformity closes down the children's desire to express themselves, even if they were so inclined. Writing a successful essay requires writing the perfect essay before the test and memorizing it word for word so it can be regurgitated during the test. History teachers avoid the lessons we can all learn from history and focus rather on memorizing names and dates and then testing on them. Leading is not encouraged or rewarded, but teamwork and leaving no student left behind is enforced. If one child cannot grasp a math problem, the whole class will slow down until he does. Every child will succeed at every subject taught. This teamwork is a great strength that we will discuss later, but this causes problems in leadership. They focus on logical thinking, which leads to their success in mathematics and physics, but nowhere in their education is there any focus on conceptual thinking or creativity.

We start with their basic problem of not being able to effectively think outside the box. The young adults who come to work are trained, or one might argue, conditioned to follow orders and execute flawlessly. They are not encouraged, let alone taught, to think laterally or even conceptually, so they and their company remains inside the proverbial box. If China is really going to "take over the world", they will have to figure this one out.

When we challenge Chinese workers to come up with innovative ideas for products, technology, or process improvement, there is typically an obvious dead silence in the room. Starting with a blank page to encourage broad thinking often ends with a blank page, or at best a replica of a page from another book. Pure and unrestricted thinking with little direction is not natural and does not yield anything useful. What is very noticeable in Chinese companies is the lack of whiteboards in conference rooms or offices. We in the West put these in rooms to encourage open thought, and you will find many Western educated people gravitating to a white board to help them think. The few white boards over here are white and remain white day after day.

So, in the search for ways to improve creativity inside the workplace, we took a look at problem solving. Problem solving requires a certain amount of creativity, even though it is not really what we are looking for, but it is a form of creativity that we can leverage.

What is fascinating is the ability of the Chinese to solve problems. What is ironic is that the same regime that drives conformity and stifles creativity has afforded the Chinese this impressive ability to solve problems.

The problems to be solved by the Chinese population are generated by the Chinese Government. The government generates hundreds of rules for the public to find ways around and solve, which in turn builds up the problem solving muscle. As you know, the general public is extremely controlled and managed. There are restrictions, such as which cities you can work in, how many children you can have, what can be said publically, and on which days you can drive your car into the city. There are also the standard rules and laws that we may find normal, such as not being allowed to run a red light or park in a no-parking zone. There are problems just waiting to be solved, while some have already been solved through teamwork and creativity.

Although this type of creativity does not translate directly into what most companies are looking for, and there is still a lot of work to be done to develop this, their problem solving ability gives us a good starting point. We can develop this into what the West would regard as thinking outside the box. We'll explore ways to solve this creativity problem later, and a lot of this leverages problem solving techniques.

II - The Chinese Priority

Large multinational corporations set up global processes that they require each region and company to follow. These processes are the result of many years of refinement around end-to-end process efficiency, tainted with a little internal control, and with a splash of political bureaucracy. But, overall, their intent is good, if you are sitting in the corporate HQ and can see the big picture. For example, companies require a purchase order to be set up in their ERP system prior to ordering, say, a box of copier paper. This purchase order ensures that when it comes time to pay the vendor, there is a good receipt against the purchase order to show that the box of paper arrived, and the vendor invoice references the purchase order so that the accounts payable group can match the invoice to the delivery and smoothly pay for the paper. It also ensures a level of internal control to make sure we are not paying for something that never arrived.

However, from the Chinese buyer's eyes, whom we will call Hu Tao, his objective is simply to get the box of paper. Payment and internal controls are not his problem, and using a purchase order seems to be a long way around just to buy a simple box of paper. So what does he do? He calls the vendor (his friend) and asks him to send a guy over with a box of paper. He then signs a delivery note and tells him to send an invoice to the accounting group. All is well in Hu Tao's eyes, and he has achieved his objective. Needless to say, when the vendor invoice arrives for payment, there is a whole lot of non-value-added rework that is done to get the invoice paid, a lot of frustration, calling, and emailing inside a large company to try and find out what happened and where the paper ended up.

The good news for Hu Tao is that this extra work is not his problem, and he is halfway through his ream of paper at this point.

This must sound very self-centered and frustrating to the Western mind, so maybe I need to step back a bit and explain the "Chinese Priority".

The Chinese Priority is centered on *oneself*. You come first above all else. From a young age you are one of many, and I mean "many", and if you don't regard yourself as the first priority, you will be lost. When people are in the professional world or out in the street by themselves, there is no room for courtesy, chivalry, or any form of selfless gesture. In a country of so many people and so few resources, if you don't look out for yourself first in a crowd, then you aren't going to survive.

Simply watching people getting onto the subway is a situation that will perfectly explain the point. The Western approach would be to allow the people in the train to climb out first and then the people on the station would walk in. This assumes that we care about the people climbing out, but the Chinese don't. The objective for Hu Tao, in this case, is to get onto the train before the four hundred people behind him trample him. So he will push onto the train before the others have climbed out, causing a totally inefficient way of exchanging places. But again, looking at efficiency from a macro level is going to get him in trouble. Efficiency has to be seen from the eyes of the individual only. What is efficient for Hu Tao is for him to push ahead on into the people coming out so he can squeeze past and get in ahead of the rest of the crowd.

In the West we would call Hu Tao badly mannered, selfish, or self-centered. But this is only a judgment from our cultural perspective. Behavior like this in the

Western world would be very noticeable and commented on, but in China this is the norm and not taken personally. People are not criticized or chastised for this. It is how they are raised and have adapted to the enormous demand for so little. The same applies to standing in line to check out at the grocery store. The general rule is that if you can't smell the person's shampoo in front of you, then you are leaving a gap big enough for someone else to slip in and pay before you. Everyone for themselves is the accepted rule of survival.

Traffic is a great way to see this in action and to help explain how the Chinese Priority differs from the West. Hu Tao is on a business trip in the U.S. and is driving along the I-35 in Dallas. He suddenly breaks hard as he approaches a long line of cars waiting impatiently to squeeze past some road construction. Cars are bumper to bumper and tempers are rising. Hu Tao simply drives onto the shoulder of the road and passes the row of cars as he swiftly moves forward to the front of the line. As the drivers in the line see him do this, they are outraged at his audacity. Some drivers who spot him in their mirror try to ease out into the shoulder to block his path. Other use familiar hand gestures to show their disapproval. And when Hu Tao gets to the front of the line and tries to merge back in, it is a battle of wills until he forces himself in.

The next week he is back in Nanjing China, and Hu Tao is driving along and comes up against a similar backlog of traffic trying to squeeze through a bottleneck caused by construction. Without a second thought (other than about himself), he drives onto the sidewalk, forcing people out of the way, and drives forward to the front of the line. As he passes the cars on his left, the Chinese drivers glance at him with indifference, but they are inspired by his ability to solve the problem. They, too, then pull out onto the sidewalk and follow him. When Hu Tao reaches the front of the line, the reaction from the other drivers is limited to wondering why they hadn't thought of that idea, and they let him into the line. Note that there is no aggression or frustration as there is in Dallas, nor is there any need for vindication. Road rage is very rare in China because the playing field is even and anything goes for everyone.

The Chinese Priority drives behavior that works well in China and in a lot of ways forms the foundation for how society works and how businesses are run. But if the Chinese want to move onto the global playing field, this behavior will need change. It will not be accepted in that arena and they will be left wondering why the referee keeps showing them the red card.

The antidote to this problem is teamwork. In stark contrast to the self-centered approach in normal society, there is an equally powerful ability to counter this with teamwork. Teams are based on relationships, and the relationships phenomenon in Asia opens up an area we can exploit to develop teams, which in turn will subdue the Chinese Priority in the workplace, but more on that later.

III - Retention

China is going through rapid growth and at the same time an urbanization of its huge population. Published inflation numbers differ from what the man in the street feels each week, and real estate prices are unrealistically high when put in the context of local salaries. All in all, there is severe pressure for people to earn more money each year. This need for more causes unimaginable staff turnover as employees search for those higher paying jobs. There are a few distinct reasons that cause their need to earn more, and it is not as simple as inflation. Many of the drivers are cultural, and unless companies find a way to retain their employees, they will continue to spend all their time training and retraining rather than becoming globally competitive organizations.

Economic

The first of these pressures is economic. This pressure on individuals and families is real, and there is a need to earn more and more each year. Most multinational companies are adjusting pay each year way above the official 3% inflation with merit increases of 8% to 10% a year. They are also looking for Western ways to structure benefits to make the whole compensation package more tax efficient and attractive. We are seeing savings plans similar to the U.S. 401-K type options showing up, as well as seeing variable bonus schemes becoming more and more popular. All these are an attempt to retain employees who are essentially getting poorer each year.

i Marriage

The second significant pressure is social and adds to the financial stress. We see this at different stages of life. Marriage is the first of these financial burdens for the groom and his parents. In China, the wedding is primarily paid for by the groom and his parents. And although the wedding is a huge ordeal and normally consists of two or three receptions in different cities, depending on where the families originate, this is not the primary financial burden.

In Chinese culture, the daughter's parents will not entertain a marriage proposal unless the young man has purchased an apartment. This ability to provide this basic need for shelter is deeply engrained in the culture and lives on strongly into this modern age. Marriage is not even contemplated until an apartment is secured, and only then is the door opened to discuss this young union. In a recent survey, it was found that 66% of prospective grooms in China buy apartments before marriage, and the rest vow to the in-laws that they will do the same within 2-4 years of getting married.

In China, a young man of twenty-five cannot afford a down payment on an apartment, so this burden falls on his parents. To put this into perspective, in a second-tier city, the average salary for a twenty-five year old with a university degree is around U.S. $10,000 per year. An average apartment of around 1,100 square feet (100 SM) with a one hour commute to the city costs around $150,000. If you want to live in the city, double that. A down payment is impossible to achieve when the cost of an acceptable apartment is fifteen times that of their annual salary. In the U.S., families of similar economic stature would typically spend around three times their annual income on a house or apartment. This disconnect between local salaries and housing is a huge problem for the young men of marrying age as well as for their parents.

While parents in the U.S. are saving desperately for future university fees, Hu Tao's parents are saving to be able to buy him an apartment to ensure that he can marry and provide a grandchild.

ii Education

Education in China has been written about quite a lot, with the focus on the pressure that Chinese parents (typically the mother) place on their child to excel at school. However, the financial aspect of this is where we will focus. Parents know that getting their child into a good school is vital for a good education, and a good school starts at kindergarten, which leads to a good middle and high school. But to get into a good kindergarten, your child needs to show ability above his or her peers. So the preparation starts very young, with music lessons, reading, writing, and numbers, all in preparation for admission to a good kindergarten.

Please meet Li Ping, a mother preparing her six-year-old son, Li Tian, for his entrance exam. She leaves him alone for 30 minutes with the hope that he will keep himself busy and focused. She needs the time alone to prepare for his entrance exam as well. Yes, they will both be going to school to demonstrate their academic ability in different ways. Today is his first of two assessments, where he will be assessed on his math and logical thinking. They set off early so as not to be late for this important day. She helps him put on his socks and shoes and makes him count to twenty in English. The Kindergarten assessors will be impressed with his English knowledge. Little do they know that it has cost her fifteen thousand dollars U.S. a year to send him to an international pre-school to make sure he socialized and that he picked up English from the age of four.

At the school, her son is taken into a separate room to be assessed, and she is led into a small classroom with a row of desks neatly lined up with three educators sitting behind them. With a short introduction about herself and her son, she spends the next five minutes giving her prepared speech on her philosophy on academics and education. She memorized this speech easily once it was written, reaching back to her own school education, where memorization was key to being successful. The man at the middle desk quizzes her on what after-school activities she has engaged her son in and how many hours a day he spends reading and playing the piano.

With little fanfare she is excused, and the next mother is walked in to take her spot in front of the group. The stress of this process is intense, but she is determined not to transfer this stress and not to let her son sense this. She sits outside and focuses on the reasons for this path down which she was pushing her son Li Tian. It is very clear that the government is not going to be able to supply any pension or social security for herself and her husband. The One Child policy has guaranteed that. They will have to rely on their own savings and hopefully their son's ability to help support them. In twenty years, with a child of his own,

Li Tian and his future wife will be heavily burdened to care for the couple's four parents. The only way Li Tian will be able afford to support his and his wife's parents will be to get to a position of power and wealth. This will be an arduous process considering the huge competition he is up against. He will have to be ahead of the pack at a very early age to get where his mother wants and needs him to go. Li Tian will be her lifetime investment, for his sake and hers.

The results arrive three weeks later, and Li Tian has been accepted into the school. Li Ping cries quietly to herself, and Li Tian merely shrugs and runs off to play with his books. Little does he know that he will have to continuously perform at a level that would allow him to remain in this school. If his grades and performance slips, he will face the pressure of the other four thousand children who had applied along with him to get into the school. He was one of the lucky one hundred who had been accepted.

When the time comes to place Li Tian into middle school, it will be time to move to a more upscale area to be closer to the best schools. They will need to upgrade their apartment, which means taking on another forty-year mortgage and starting again with this burden. So again they start to feel the financial pressure as they take on higher mortgage payments.

Now you may be saying to yourself that this need to live in a good suburb with good schools is normal in the U.S. and that we all suffer under the same financial strain to educate our children in the best schools possible, but in China this is different. The duty the parents feel to have to educated their child at the highest level is huge. It is a dedication way beyond anything we see in the West. The grandparents are driving the parents, and the parents, who have lived through the same school pressure, continue the tradition, or even more, they continue the *necessity* to have their kids be the best at everything.

When I discussed this phenomena with a local Chinese mother, she was telling me how she was starting to perfect her "disappointed face". This is the same face that her mother had used against her when she did not succeed in a test or failed to get an A+. The fear of this expression of disappointment is deeply engrained in all Chinese children, and even grown adults still fear this simple look that their mothers will give them when they are not meeting her expectations. So this young mother of a six year old was working on this facial expression of disappointment that would drive her son forward in life through the absolute fear of having to see that dreaded expression.

This obsession to have their children perform at the top of their class, be it piano, kindergarten, or 10th grade, comes from a deep-rooted drive to start out and remain ahead of your peers. Along with the loathed "face of disappointment" there is the family name to uphold. Letting down your parents and your father's name brings great shame to the family, and no one wants to be the cause of that, ever.

Companies, trying to retain employees, need to be aware of the financial pressures both marriage and educating their children has on them. Understanding the various stages of life which their staff members are at will improve the odds of dealing with the challenge head-on rather than being surprised by yet another resignation to find more pay.

As the One-Child policy is phased out and families start having two children, this burden will double. The One Child policy was put in place in 1979, where couples in urban areas were restricted to one child, whereas families living in rural areas could have more than one child to support their farms and livelihood. This policy was intended to be for one generation, and now that the children of the One Child policy are getting married, the regulation is being relaxed and these children may now have two children of their own once they have applied to the government for approval. So we will start to see the financial burden grow as two children are walked through the school process.

iii Keeping up with the Joneses

The third social pressure is interesting, and I am not sure I understand it very well in China's economic situation. We would call it, "Keeping up with the Joneses," in South Africa. In urban China, it is very important to show with your possessions your achievements and status. Your home, your watch, and your car are all good ways to distinguish your status and achievements from those of your friends and neighbors. It is quite common for a middle-class person to buy an imported car (Yes, a Buick is a very cool car over here.) and park it at home for weekend viewing and driving. During the week, the owner of that car is just the next guy riding his bicycle or moped to work, but on the weekend, he drives it to meet friends at the lake or mall and flashes it around. What is fascinating to me is that the parking garage space in typical apartment buildings are almost the same cost per square meter as the actual apartment, and yet people still feel it is worth the expense. Cars are seen as the ultimate vehicle to inform your neighbors of the status you have reached; please pardon the pun. The car as the status symbol is normally limited to people who can almost afford them halfway through their careers. The younger crowd will use watches, high fashion clothes, and accessories to define their status and separate themselves from their peers.

■■

Having traveled from New York, Joan spent her second day in Shanghai feeling worse from jet lag than the day before. However, the thought of bargains at the fake market spurred her on. As she walked underground into what looked like a huge market area split into hundreds of small stores, she wondered if they were as cheap as she had heard from her Chinese friends. The noise grew, as she wandered closer to the first gauntlet of storekeepers standing in front of their little shop fronts. The chatter started as they saw her approach.

"Best price, what you look. Come see, what you need. I give you good price, first customer price. Gucci, Prada, what you like."

The touching on her arm to stop her moving past the store annoyed her, and the relentless calling, coaxing, and insistence was deafening and a little frightening.

She moved through the first stores quickly as advised, because these were at the front with prime tourist advantage and would charge more than those at the back.

"Jimmy Choo, Calvin Klein, what you like? I give you good price. Come look, very good bag."

She made it through the first hall of stalls, making a quick right to avoid the next group that had already heard the escalating chatter and were ready for her. She crossed over two rows and headed toward the back.

"Armani, Hugo Boss, come take look. Good price. Very cheap. Very good quality."

Skipping over one aisle was a good move, as she had found a slightly quieter group of shops where the assistants were all chatting amongst themselves. And there is was — the *Gucci-Bamboo* bag she was looking for.

"Come look. Good price. Come inside. Take look."

She walked into a ten-by-ten-foot stall full with designer bags from floor to ceiling.

"How much is this one?" Joan asked.
"For you, special price, five thousand."
"Five thousand Chinese Yuan?"
"Dui."

Joan did the math quickly and figured that the price was $800. *Not bad for a bag that would cost $4,500 back home, but is it real?* She took a close look at the stitching and the inside of the bag. The handle felt real and it had the right look, but the outside felt wrong. It was too glossy or smooth, and the chain on the side looked cheap.

"This is not real; this feels fake," she questioned the store assistant.
"I have better fake one. Wait, I go find."

The store assistant brought back three others from the store across the way. The first one was seven thousand Yuan and looked better, but still not quite right. The next one was similar, but the one for fifteen thousand Yuan could have been the real deal.

That's $2,000 for what was as close to being the genuine article as you would ever find, compared to a retail price in New York of $4,500. But $2,000 was a lot to pay for a fake. She wondered what the cheaper one was like and had a look at the one across the table. It was still very close, and no one could tell from a distance. Nor could they possible tell unless they started digging in her bag. Maybe her friends would know, but they would laugh. That one for fifteen thousand Yuan seemed like the best option.

"I will give you eight thousand Yuan for that one," she offered.

The shop assistant, understanding that she had Joan on the hook, leaned over and picked up her calculator. She typed in nine thousand, five hundred Yuan and showed it to Joan. Joan took the calculator from her and typed in eight thousand, five hundred Yuan, but the young lady just laughed a mocking laugh. She took the calculator and re-typed Nine thousand, five hundred Yuan. Joan glanced over to the shop across the aisle, where she noticed a similar bag and decided to explore her options. So she shook her head and said, "Eight thousand five hundred Yuan," and started to walk away toward the other shop.

"Wait! Wait! I give you good price. You my first customer and good luck to make deal. I give you for nine thousand Yuan, and I give you small bag for luck."

Joan smiled to herself and felt that sense of accomplishment at having won the famous Chinese game of haggle. She paid the lady, took her bag, and wandered off feeling very proud of her bargaining ability.
The shop assistant put the cash into the drawer and looked up to see her friends from the next store walking in. They laughed when she told them how much Joan had paid for a five hundred Chinese Yuan bag. And she smiled to herself with a sense of accomplishment at having won the famous Chinese game of haggle!

Across the road, Li Ping was ready to enter the big league and finally get herself the same Gucci Bamboo handbag as Joan. All her friends had a Gucci, so why shouldn't she?

Let's be honest, she said to herself. *My friends are starting to doubt my sense of style, and I can see them looking at my old bag and whispering amongst themselves.*
She would just have to find a way to buy this one, whatever it took.

Shanghai is full of shopping malls that carry designer brand articles, but the authentic article only. No fakes are in the malls, and absolutely no bargaining is allowed, as much as you would like to try.

As Li Ping got into the taxi, she wondered if it was worth trying at the fake market. Maybe there was an absolutely foolproof fake that no one could discern as being anything other than the authentic article. And just maybe the price would be within her reach. But in her heart she knew that the average Chinese eye had been trained from birth to spot a fake at a hundred yards. When only one out of five items available is the real deal, this skill is learned early, because the mistake of buying a fake of any retail item can be an expensive one. Parents educate their children from a young age on how to spot problems with merchandise. Lessons are taught on how to distinguish oranges and apples that have been injected with water to make them plumper and weigh more, to distinguish shoes where the designer label is not quite straight on the sole of the shoe.

There was no way a fake would do the trick, plus, she would not be caught dead in the fake market. Being spotted in there could put in question everything she wore and everything she carried for next few years. That would be an expensive mistake.

So off she went to the mall and right into the Gucci store. There, she saw that wonderful Bamboo-Gucci she had been dreaming of and looking at on the Internet. As one would imagine, there were no prices displayed, and it was assumed that if you had to ask, you were probably in the wrong shop. She walked over and picked the bag up. The cable securing it became taught as she pulled it lovingly toward her side. It was perfect, and it said exactly what she needed it to say.

"Duo shao qian?" she asked.

"Thirty thousand Yuan," the clerk answered in English, which is $4,500.
Li Ping's heart sank, and her credit card hid itself deeper in her wallet.
This would stretch her beyond what she could afford, even if she used that final credit card she kept for emergencies. Then she remembered that her friend, Ling Ling, was going to Boston for a conference with her company. Maybe she could buy one in the U.S. and bring it back to China for her. Yes, that will work, and then she will have an even better quality that any bought in China — or at least it would feel that way.
Reluctantly letting go of the bag and taking a sudden bogus cell phone call, she exited the store, trying to retain some of her dignity.

Sadly, there are many Li Pings in China not only trying to keep up to date with the latest fashions but also the latest technology and convenience. In the eastern and more modern cities, people are focusing on high fashion and the latest Apple technology, but in the western part of China, where urbanization and modernization has just started, there is a focus on convenience. Items like washing machines and air conditioners are being made and sold by the million each year. The demand for microwaves and refrigerators takes the place of handbags and technology, but nevertheless the need for more and more is moving quickly from China's eastern districts to the rural areas in the west.

When you consider the financial pressure that the urban Chinese people feel, whether it is having to buy their son an apartment, moving to a better school district every four years, or trying to keep up with the Joneses, you can start to understand the job retention problem companies have. We all have the desire to make more and improve our standard of living, but the Chinese have extra financial burdens that are driven by norms so embedded in their culture that they are impossible to ignore. These drivers result in unusual financial pressure, which forces them to constantly be looking for better paying jobs and more senior positions.

On top of this push from the financial and social pressure, there is also a pull. This is a pull by headhunters to attract them to new and higher-paying opportunities. In the West, we get tired of our boss or company, put together a resume, and send it to agencies or directly to companies for review. We are at the mercy of the prospective employers as the supply is much greater than the demand. In China, however, the average professional, in my experience, receives at least one call a week from headhunters. One might expect this at the senior manager or specialist level, but these calls start after only one year of work experience.

Headhunters buy companies' internal phone lists from unscrupulous employees and start calling everyone on the list. They know that their ability to attract people to other jobs is quite easy in this environment. The money they can earn from the commission and the volume of people they can move makes this a highly profitable profession. The reason they can move people so easily from job to job is that the market has valued the risk of moving from one job to another at a 30% pay raise. Generally, if a Chinese company replaces a former employee with a similarly skilled and experienced person, they will pay a 30% premium. This premium is what the market has determined as an acceptable pay raise to justify the risk associated with moving to a new company. Turnover of employees is expensive in any country when you consider the recruiting fees, learning curve time, and loss of productivity, but in China, the 30% additional base salary is permanent and moves your base pay higher and higher. It also causes problems with equality amongst employees. Salaries are not regarded as very confidential here, and most employees will talk about them with each other. When a new person is hired with the premium, the current staff feels cheated and either asks for a raise to match it or they start to look around for an offer at the premium.

iv Allegiance

The final key factor in employee retention is a simple fact that took me awhile to realize and understand. It is the concept of allegiance. Thirty years ago, if you worked in a large corporation in the USA or Europe, you were locked in for life. You were a fixed asset of the company, which depreciated over thirty years at the same pace your pension plan appreciated. You were pretty much guaranteed a job unless you trashed the CEO's office. Even then, rather than fire you, they'd probably just send you for counseling and move you to the basement.

Then, along came the problem of under-funded pension plans, the shift to the 401-k, and defined contribution plans. Suddenly, there wasn't a strong reason such as a pension plan to hold people to their company. The loyalty, if that's what it was, was weakened. Then came the era of mergers and of acquisition activities in the 1990s and 2000s, and people very quickly began to understand that the loyalty was one-sided. One day you're sitting at your desk feeling very safe, and the next day the morning news tells you that your company has just been bought out and that they expect to save millions through synergies.

Unfortunately, you would be one of those *synergies*. With all this movement between companies, the 401-k rollover process was introduced to help people avoid spending their savings after each separation.

As word spread that the companies were turning over CEOs and senior executives as often as they were closing the books, they realized that the loyalty of the Board to the CEO wasn't very strong, which implied that the CEO's loyalty to the company was equally weak. This weakening allegiance spread throughout the organization, and U.S. companies entered a state that left them vulnerable to their employees and suffering from the lack of passion and strength that comes with a strong corporate family.

Like supply and demand, the balance was defined as, "My loyalty to the company is as strong as the company's loyalty to me." Pink slips and layoffs in the recession sealed the deal, and the passion for the company died. Now we see companies full of temporary workers and temporary CEOs keeping it together with the glue of stock options for the senior executives and the fear of being unemployed at the lower end. This is a synthetic type of loyalty that is causing long-term issues in the West.

In China, they haven't been down the pension and 401-k path yet. Nor have they seen the mergers and acquisitions that the U.S. or the EU has seen. The reliance on the government pension promise is now a concern, and the companies are responding with their saving plans and stock options. These larger companies are stable and Chinese owned. However, the allegiance is still not to the company. The company doesn't promise anything to the employees. There isn't a sense of company pride or strong values in Chinese companies.

"We work for the boss, not for the company," she said.

Then the light bulb came on. The allegiance is not to the company; it is to the boss. Retain the boss and you retain the employees.

Business is conducted through relationships in China. This is what greases the wheels of the economy. So, it stands to reason that the work force is built around close relationships as well. Rather than stock options and the fear of being unemployed being the glue that holds the company together, we have a hierarchical allegiance keeping it together in China. This is a weakness for companies that are unable to retain their managers, because their people tend to follow them to the next company. It is also a strength that can be leveraged if you are able to retain them. It has also proven to be an advantage over the West, where in the West there is no allegiance to the company or the boss. At least in China we have an allegiance to the boss with which to work.

IV - Imagination

The next gap we see in China's leadership challenge is the limited imagination. Leaders in China, as well as senior managers, really struggle to draw a picture of the future for their group. Some, when pushed to develop a vision, will come back with a long list of process-improvement ideas rather than the end state. Drawing a picture of the path is much easier and more tangible than drawing a picture of the destination. Part of the problem is that they don't understand the need for this effort. They don't see the value of the exercise. If they struggle to imagine the vision, as it is conceptual and intangible, why would their staff be able to understand it? Most have never seen the full cycle from the vision to achieving the vision, and they don't get how powerful this process can be. Or perhaps they don't believe they could ever get their staff to listen to them without them falling asleep. If he can barely buy into this long-term approach himself, then how could he ever get his staff to buy into it?
So where I am on this is that most managers are quite capable of putting this together but don't see the value in this because it is too long term and would have no effect on their groups even if it was developed and explained to them.

So what I have typically seen is a poor attempt to build a set of goals formatted to look like a vision to please senior management. However, the selling of the vision is skipped and morphs quickly into a list of ideas for improvement that gives the group value-added action items to work on. The vision typically stays in the expats office and is used to justify the actions being taken rather than inspiring the site. Either way, the group moves forward, just for a different reason. That's not bad, but it's not as good as it could get.

V - Organizational development

Careers for professionals in the Chinese work environment are very vertical. They pick a sub area of their profession and slide in at the lowest level right out of university. Then they work very hard to learn what they can within their box. When they hand off work to the next step of the process, they stick the hand out of the box briefly to pass this information on to the next guy. Responsibility for that parcel passes on at the same time, and they settle back down in the box to process.

Unfortunately, this limits their exposure to downstream processes and potential learning. They work hard on the relationship with their immediate boss, who has absolute power over their careers. They are conditioned to accept what the boss feels is right.

When I first started discussing individual development and career plans, the first question I asked was, "Where do you want to be in 3-5 years?" The answer invariably was, "That's up to you, Boss."

Wow! I was amazed, firstly at the blind trust they put in their managers and, secondly, at how this must be so uninspiring and frustrating. As I started to work with managers and ask them how they managed careers for their people, the answer was deafening — deafening silence. There was no understanding of the concept of career planning. The general agreement was that employees worked in their job until a job opened up after someone left or they were finally lured away by headhunters. Some high-potential people would spend years in the same routine job, especially if they didn't have a good relationship with their boss.

Career direction is accepted as purely vertical within their function. As I discovered in discussions with many people, their passion was to become the absolute expert in their small area. Some would commit years to this goal and justify it to themselves each time a promotion didn't come their way. Career paths are decided early on in school. For example, if you study international trade, you start in the import/export group, and you are expected to stay in that part of the company all your life. Parents are key drivers to this. They believe that *time* is the answer to promotions. So the longer you stay in one specific function, the better your chances to rise up in the organization. Unfortunately, if you are offered an opportunity to move into the shipping team, this is regarded as a sideways move and will do nothing other than slow down the vertical progression.

I guess it is an effective arrangement when the employee expects nothing and the managers have nothing to offer. This limitation will be felt quite clearly when these employees start to play in the global game and they are found to be wanting on breadth. Western standards demand broad cross-functional understanding with depth, but with plenty of breadth. The speed of conference room discussions and business meetings does not allow for consultation with various functions to be sure of an answer or to drive a conversation forward.

If you have ever met with a delegation from Asia, they always arrive in large groups with specialists from each function to support the meeting. I have always found it interesting to sit across the table from seven Chinese businessmen with only myself on this side of the table. Most of the discussion is held between the Chinese groups as they consult across functions to reach the decision they need in order to move the discussion forward. This is not efficient enough for the world stage and will hold them back.

Consequently, one of the major challenges but most rewarding exercises we will discuss later is how we can unlock the career and growth concept, both for the employees and for the managers.

VI – Motivation

This area of the Chinese culture is as simple as it is complex. Trying to help an individual reach his or her full potential must start with understanding what motivates them. I happened across the answer to this mystery while I was exploring the dark area of kickback fraud in China and how I could strengthen internal controls.

When a company puts in place basic internal controls to reduce the risk of fraud, it relies on two very basic elements that are intrinsic to the success of these controls. One is called *segregation of duties* and the other is *the whistle blower*. Segregation of duties simply means that the guy who can sign the checks should not have control over the check book. If he did want to steal money from the company, he would have to partner up with the guy who keeps the checkbook. Internal controls rely on the fact that people will not collude in an attempt to commit fraud.

The second basic assumption is that people will naturally tell on each other. In Western culture, there is a built-in sense of what is right and wrong. There is also an assumed responsibility that if you notice something illegal or suspicious you should report it. In China, there is a different definition of what is ethical and unethical in business; however, the real issue is the sense of responsibility.

As we started to find more and more cases of fraud where everyone knew it was going on but no one was telling, I became very frustrated because I was realizing that I could not rely on this one basic component of control — that the whistle blowers exist in China.

In an attempt to understand the reason people refused to be whistle blowers, I stumbled upon the primary motivator for the Chinese who I worked with. The answer I found was surprisingly simple, so I asked someone to validate my learning. She seemed a little perplexed as to why I didn't already understand this. After all, this was as obvious to her as why they use chop sticks instead of a knife and fork.

The answer to the big mystery is the attitude of, "What's in it for me?" The primary motivator and key question used for those moments of indecision is this:

When they come across someone receiving a kickback under the table and the company rules require them to report it, they ask themselves this question, "What's in it for me?"

Here is an awful but true story that amplifies the strength of this motivator.

Little two-year-old Xioa Yue Yue was playing outside in a small back shopping street when a truck ran into her and then ran over her. The driver paused for a moment and then drove on again, crushing her little body with his back wheel. For seven minutes people in the street walked right past her, and drivers of cars didn't stop to help this little girl bleeding on the road. No one stopped to help or even to call for help. A little later, another vehicle ran over her again. After eighteen people had either driven or walked past her, leaving her to die on the road, an old street sweeper stopped to help the girl who later died of her injuries.

China has video cameras on every street corner, and this particular video made it out and went viral. The press went into a frenzy and questioned the humanity of the Chinese. The local Chinese blogs were crammed with damnation against the eighteen people who had walked by, blaming them for an unconscionable act.

Along with the rest of the world, I wondered why no one stopped and how heartless they could be, especially with a little two year old who was so helpless? My belief is that each one of the eighteen people asked themselves the same question, "What's in it for me to stop and help?" The answer was quite simply, "Nothing positive."

In 2006, there was a case where a lady had fallen over in the street. A gentleman called Peng Yu had stopped to help the lady and had taken her to the hospital. She then sued him for actually causing her injuries, and the court upheld her claim. This ruling became very well-known and drove people to be afraid to help someone in case they were implicated in the event. My assumption is that these eighteen people knew of this famous case and answered the question "What's in it for me?" based on that.

This story is awful, and millions of Chinese struggled to understand this and questioned what they themselves would have done had they been there. If nothing else, this event demonstrates how powerful this motivator can be to the Chinese.

If you choose to Google the video of little Xiao Yue Yue, you do so at your own peril, for it is very painful to watch.

Understanding this primary motivator is vital to be able to tackle the management gaps defined above. This ultimate question of, "What's in it for me?" is typically answered with, "Money," in the West. However, in the East, money is not the answer, which seems contrary to the discussion on social and economic pressure above. Money, of course, can be useful and can help bribe your way out of a lot of trouble, but in the context on the work environment, I have found that money is not at the top of the list. In fact, across the board, this was not even in the top two.

I was intrigued to find out that although the motivation question was simple, the answers were much more complex. For instance, the number-one motivator by employees in my world was, *Recognition by management.* Second was *Career development & opportunities.* The third was *Money,* and finally *Work Life Balance.* One could argue that *Career Development and Opportunities* translates into money ultimately, but there is something more here than purely money, but more on that later.

The concept of *Recognition by Management* started to attract my attention when more and more people were posting this at the top of their *motivators.* I had asked everyone to list their top five motivators so that we, as managers, could make sure we are pushing the right buttons to get the best performance out of people. As a company, we had imported the U.S. approach to solving employee unhappiness by assuming that money could fix this as it does in the U.S. It is fairly common for the resignation letter of a key employee to be nothing more than the starting point for salary negotiations. Even if it isn't, it makes the mangers feel that they did all they could to retain the employee by offering them better pay. In China, the resignation letter is the final step in a process that can't simply be fixed by money. International companies have continued to combat the loss of key employees with more attractive packages to make them stay, but they have been missing the mark on this. What we have learned is that the money aspect of the problem was already solved by the new job offer of the prospective new employer. What needed taking care of were the top two or three motivators, such as management recognition and career potential.

Unfortunately, these are difficult to effectively respond to when you are looking over a letter of resignation.

We will discuss these motivators in more depth later. Suffice to say, the top retention motivator of "Recognition by Management" can be defined in the same way most people have explained it to me. It was the need to be recognized for successes, small and large, in a way that earned them points toward that next opportunity in their career or perhaps an exposure opportunity. It was not about public acknowledgment that gave them bragging rights — far from it. In fact, if you read about the Chinese culture, you will know to be very careful not to congratulate or bolster their egos in front of their peers. They hate to be publically made to stand out from their peers. They find it embarrassing to be separated by being held above their friends and co-workers. We must remember their schooling where showing leadership and standing out from the crowd was strongly discouraged.

The other aspect of *Recognition by Management* that I believe is the defining reason for the power of this is the parent/child relationship. A parent, particularly a mother, spends a lot of energy encouraging her child throughout school. She also has a significant impact when the child causes disappointment. The child is conditioned to excel in order to gain praise from his mother. This recognition is vital during the school days and right through university. It acts as the primary motivator for a successful academic performance. When the student moves into the professional world, his parents seems further away and are not aware of specific work-related achievements as they would have been during school with test scores being brought home. So the young adults still crave the recognition to replace their parents as a source of motivation through their early careers. It is interesting that even long into people's careers there is still this need for recognition by management. The motivator remains an inbuilt need encoded throughout the school years.

Another form of motivation we need to understand is the concept that nothing is ever wasted in China. Those of you who have ever eaten a typical Chinese meal will know that when it comes to the parts of the animal they eat, nothing is wasted. If it moves, it is fair game for the table. The head, the feet, and everything in-between, of all the animals, fish, and certain long slithery reptiles, are considered nutrition. (Okay, snakes and fish don't technically have feet, but if they did . . .)

Another typical area of waste in our new green world is that of trash recycling. I was asked more than once why we didn't separate our paper from our tin cans in the office to help the environment. My answer was always the same, "I'm protecting the poor."

Every company that started separating and shipping off to recycling centers in China was putting a few families back on the street because their livelihood was taken away. At night, when tons of waste is dragged out of the offices in large black bags, the "recyclers" wait to grab these bags and start to separate out the treasure into high and low value. Every can is squashed, every page saved, and every piece of plastic is carted off through the night to informal recycling centers where these families are paid on weight. They push large carts around town, piled so high with their spoils that they can't see where they are going. They collect their few RMB and return the next day to do it all over again.

Nothing is ever wasted in China because there isn't enough to go around. Resources for such a large population have always been in short supply, be it food, clothing, or arable land. Even today, as the economy is really running hard, you will still find impromptu vegetable gardens on the side of public roads and highways. Every patch of fertile land close to water will be quietly hand tilled and seeds sown at night. Every scrap of metal, plastic bottle, or article of secondhand clothing is recovered quickly and sold further west to those more in need or recycled to make something else. When it comes to reusing, this country is incredibly "green" compared to the lazy West.

Commodities that are equally precious and definitely not wasted are *time and energy*. The measure of *time and energy* is *value add*. If the activity that needs to be performed does not add any value, then it won't be done. So if you want to motivate someone to do something, you need to start by explaining the value in doing it. It is not enough to simply explain that these are the rules and that this is the way the company wants it done. This may get it done once, while you are watching, but when you check back in a few weeks, you will find that the process stopped as soon as you left the room. The only way to make sustainable change like this is to put in the effort to explain and convince them that there is real value in doing this. You need to factor in the question of, "What's in it for me?" as part of the offering, but when you get creative, there are ways to make the link between company values and personal needs. I don't want to give the impression that the company only runs well if you can satisfy each individual's need to see his own value in each task that needs to be done. This isn't the case at all. These are smart people who understand that they are running a company that operates as a whole; however, if you want direct and sustainable change, then you need to explain the value.

You can, of course, use power to force action by threatening their job if they don't follow the requirements. This is certainly effective if you have the ability to catch those not complying and are willing to fire a few. If you don't police this rule, then they will test your vigilance. If you fail to be watching, they will immediately disregard the rule. However, if you can police and punish, you can be very successful in implementing change and new rules. This is how drivers are motivated to obey traffic rules. The police have installed close to a hundred thousand cameras in an average city to enforce security and traffic rules. In one particular city there are four cameras at each and every traffic light, constantly taking pictures and sending out traffic fines. Then there are separate cameras monitoring no-parking zones, speeding, and crossing double lines. These photos are posted to your private web account registered to the vehicle, and the driver receives a text message when he has been fined. These fines can pile up over the year, but you are not able to renew the vehicle license until all the fines have been paid. This is a pretty strong motivator to obey the traffic rules. It's an amazing contrast to see cars perfectly stopped six feet before the stop line to avoid triggering the cameras, but at the same time, twenty-five unlicensed scooters will drive right through the same red light because the cameras can't identify their unlicensed scooters.

Although this motivator of "catch and punish" is strong, it also offers great possibilities for those who are creative in nature. Camera blind spots are blogged about and shared on forums, and "experts" offer advice on how to negotiate with the traffic department for a lesser fine based on the ambiguous nature of a particular photo. An industry booms around high definition cameras for the police so that faces can be identified by a camera two hundred yards away. Custom-made mirrors that can be attached to the license plates to simulate a legitimate reflection on the camera lens when it takes the photo are sold online. It is a constant battle between the police and the drivers as they jockey for supremacy in this field.

Minimizing the waste of time or effort is a key motivator that can be used in a positive way. When we enter the realm of efficiency and productivity, we have a perfect stage for developing the best in the world. At the end of the day, every process will be naturally eliminated of anything that is not value-added to the end product. If we start at A and want to end at C, typically the stop at B is simply eliminated. There is an in-built sensitivity to waste, and the Chinese worker will automatically challenge the value of each step in the process. If it holds no value, it will be skipped. If it is a governance or control step that adds value to the corporate office, it will be skipped unless compliance is policed and punished, or the value of the control to the company and the employee is well explained and brought into play.

Let's continue our discussion on traffic. If a driver misses an exit on the highway, he has two choices. He can keep driving to the next exit, turn around, and come back to take the right exit. This option is full of non-value-added activity. To begin with, time and gas is wasted. His second option is to hit the brakes hard and drive in reverse the two hundred yards against oncoming traffic to the exit he missed. This option is better when weighed against the value-added rule and he will immediately stop on the highway. Then there is the question of reversing against traffic. This is a question of risk versus reward. It is the risk of being caught by the police versus the time and fuel savings. Note that in the West the factor of annoying the other drivers and putting them in danger would be a big one. In China, as explained earlier, this is really not a consideration. To the screech of brakes and warning horns, he will reverse the two hundred yards and accept his value with satisfaction as he drives down the ramp. Sadly, this example is seen every day when I drive home. Really, I mean *every day*.

An area we struggle with is motivation. For efficient processes, motivation is typically based on the individual's assessment of risk and reward and not that of the full end-to-end process. One of the huge challenges, when we looked at using the time and effort motivators, was to reenforce the risk to everyone in the chain, not just to themselves. This was shown in 2008 when a milk producer was illegally adding melamine to artificially inflate the protein level. He wasn't thinking about the babies who would drink this milk and the hospitalization of over fifty thousand babies.

VII – Summary

We have some real problems in China that can prove to be challenging to overcome. The initial look revealed that there was a huge gap in creativity, which may not have shown up in a business setting but was definitely not lacking in other areas of their lives. The world's perception of China is that they are copiers and unable to come up with innovative ideas on their own. The intellectual property crisis in China stands testament, where hundreds of court cases each year are targeting Chinese companies who are stealing ideas from outside of China. This reputation only cements the view that they are unable to be original themselves. My focus is smaller than these larger IP issues; nonetheless, the office environment seems to follow the same trend.

The huge problem of employee retention in the economy is one that seems insurmountable until the economy cools off. Somehow, I think the cooling off of the Chinese economy will not be for many years, considering the percentage of the population and geographic area that is not yet developed. It is almost like the U.S. was before the railroads made it out West. There is massive potential still to be exploited. Retaining people in companies is going to be key in developing ways that will allow them to work in the global arena. Without slowing the staff turnover rate, companies will always be in firefighting mode as they try to train and retrain rather than develop people and leaders who they are going to need down the road.

In the area of leadership encompassing areas of vision to developing people, when you peek into that box and say hello, there is an echo. And finally is the most basic of all, the engine that makes it all work — motivation. There is plenty of motivation, but understanding it and being able to steer with it proves to be difficult. However, once you have cracked the code and understand the real motivators of the Chinese worker, the potential is awesome.

WHAT *DO* WE HAVE TO WORK WITH?

The positive aspects of the Chinese people I have met and worked with are overwhelming. It was this reason that really drove me to find a solution for the gaps we talked about above. There are so many impressive qualities that shout out at you that you can easily forget about the challenges and ride the wave that the rest of the country is riding. Running this country, as they do, within the Chinese way, is working and cannot be faulted when viewed domestically, but in order to truly compete with international companies and reach their full potential, this long list of positive qualities can be seen as a great base and starting point to close the gap.

I - Eagerness to Learn.

The list of positive qualities is long, but I think one of my favorite qualities of the Chinese is their eagerness to learn.
I started my first day in the office with a small staff meeting to get to know everyone. In their eyes, the big boss from the U.S. had arrived, and there was no telling what life would be like under this new regime. All heads were still and eyes carefully cast downward to avoid confrontation and to show respect. They were there to take orders and to serve. This was the message I received from their body language. However, I was sadly mistaken. I introduced myself and my background and quickly opened the floor up for any questions. One of the senior accountants had clearly been selected to ask the only question they had, "What can you teach us?"

 This was said in such a positive and hopeful way, and there was no doubt that this was a genuine appeal to me to help them learn and grow. As it turned out, they were extremely excited to find out that someone from the head office was coming over and had enough technical background to really help them improve their skills. Whenever I tell this story, I always wonder what the first question would have been in the U.S. It probably would have been, "What is your plan to reduce our heavy workload and pay us more?"

This attitude is so contrary that it is hard to image how the U.S. reached the standards they did. But I guess that after a couple of generations of *plenty* you should expect this entitlement attitude amongst those in the West. This difference in attitude is the core reason why the U.S. will lose to the Chinese over time.

During candidate interviews, I have always looked for one basic quality: Do they have the motivation and ability to learn? This comes as part of the standard package in China. In fact, it's so fundamental to their needs that it became a key part of *our* interview selling approach when trying to attract the best employees. Companies who offer development plans that keep them constantly on the learning curve can quickly develop a reputation in the top universities for being an employer of choice. The typical Chinese company does not put much emphasis on career development, let alone simple job study and learning. They are there to perform their duties accurately and with as little support as possible. Average employees can easily spend years in a fairly routine position without any opportunity being given to them. When companies start to talk about careers and development as part of the package, there will be a line at the door for the best candidates. Those companies that have succeeded at this have reached the point where getting into these companies is only done through recommendation. As jobs open up, current employees will bring their friends and associates forward for the roles. This process helps breed a very strong workforce, because friends are only recommended to the company if they are sure they will succeed and will not cause any negative impact to the referring employee's reputation.

i. Continuous learning

The continuous learner in the Chinese mindset stems from their upbringing and the relentless pursuit of success by their parents. From a young age they are pushed to learn and achieve the best academic success possible. They are sent to the best universities that will have them, with the hope that they will find a good job with good prospects. However, one would imagine that once these kids have moved out of their homes they would be free of the parents' pressure, but they continue to feel the need to better themselves for their parents' sake. Advanced studies and multiple certifications are normal and expected as part of your first ten years at work. Perhaps the parents still compete with each other over how successful their children are and they continue to pressure them. Sadly, a lot of the certifications that parents encourage their children to obtain carry no weight in their career advancement. The value that they add within the company on a day-to-day basis will advance them three times faster than another certification will. That said, there is value in certifications if you choose to leave the company and apply elsewhere, because the resume is all you have to get you into the door for that first interview. At that stage your resume is being compared to many others, and the length of your academic achievements is very carefully considered.

ii The ability to learn

Along with their eagerness to learn comes the ability to learn. Of all the employees I have worked with around the world, the Chinese people have far outpaced everyone else. This ability to learn is of course based on their intellectual or academic ability, which has been conditioned by constant learning throughout their lives. However, the difference I have seen is *how* they apply themselves to the task of learning. The dedication and absolute concentration on the task must contribute significantly to the speed with which they pick up the knowledge or process. This can be noticed very easily in an office environment where there is absolute silence during periods of time pressure or importance. No one is talking, and you won't find that small group of slackers. Then, lunch hour comes around and the noise is deafening as they eat and socialize and yell across the room in a happy and relaxed environment. If there is fifteen minutes left before the end of lunch, you will often find people fast asleep with their heads on their desks, taking what we might call a "Power nap". Then work starts again and the intense concentration and focus starts all over.

Behind this speed of learning is also the drive to succeed and the fear of failure. I am sure they are trying not to picture their mother's disappointed face as they strive for perfection. Making mistakes is very difficult for the Chinese to endure. I say "endure" because it is the process of admitting their mistakes and the subsequent embarrassment of failure that causes their pain. The expectations they have of themselves and the expectations their boss has of them is very obvious and is a big driver to their fast learning. The shame of making mistakes is important to understand as a manager in China, because the risk of mistakes being swept under the carpet is very high. The risk-versus-reward assessment can result in the chance of getting caught being much lower than the "reward" of being embarrassed by their supervisor. Creating an open environment and culture where mistakes are tolerated, to an extent, is a challenge for any Western company. The good news is that once this environment is achieved, you will find that the Western management's expectations, although high, are always lower than the Chinese employee's expectations of themselves. So the buffer zone between the two levels of expectations is very useful for managing operational or process risk in a company.

iii Operations

There is one limitation to the learning ability that should be mentioned. That is how it relates to the operation. Routine processes and repetitive work is what is learned very quickly. That is not to say that these are simple processes. To the contrary, these processes can be extremely complex and detailed, and they will be learned and followed with accuracy and efficiency second to none. However, if the process fails because an input is wrong or a new variable comes into play, then the wheels can fall off. The ability to react and fix a new problem requires a certain level of flexibility and creativity. The flexibility is not a problem and is abundant in most, because the change in process or situation is immediately seen as an opportunity to learn something new. However, the creativity to come up with a solution is where the trouble starts. In areas of creativity, to solve a problem, the *value add* question kicks in, and often a solution is proposed that is very local. The person involved solves it for himself, but the imagination to see further down the line and predict the impact that this solution may have on their peers or outside partners further downstream is lacking. This is not to say that the ability and imagination is not there, but the willingness to put in the extra effort to help a partner avoid a problem down the line is typically just not there.

The huge advantage of a team of quick learners is that they reach maturity on the learning curve earlier and can start adding value sooner. They are also more consistent in their ability to execute accurately and efficiently, which also allows more time in the month to work on value-added projects or process improvements. Sadly, many employees will dedicate most of their spare time to improving their internal process and not focus on the end-to-end process. They also steer away from using this time to develop value-added ideas, as this is not a natural ability and they don't find it very rewarding.

II - Teamwork

The area that I have found very positive and satisfying to witness is teamwork. In contrast to what I have said about the self-centered approach to life, teamwork in the Chinese work environment is quite amazing to watch. There is a prerequisite that the team takes the time to form a strong bond. This takes time in this culture, but spending ten hours a day together gets you there quickly, setting common goals for a team where they feel that success or failure together is vital to establishing the environment where this teamwork works.

Imagine a team working side by side, and suddenly there is a break in one team member's process. The pressure to meet the deadline is there, and working on the solution alone would take too much time. The "alarm" is sounded, and all of a sudden there are seven people huddled around a cubicle working on the problem. The noise is intense, and three discussions are concurrent, but the goal is clear. After twenty minutes of various people leaning over and driving the mouse, the glitch is fixed, the people have dispersed, and the deafening silence of concentration resumes. You have to simply stand there and wonder if you dare ask how it was fixed or just trust them and walk away.

We see a similar approach to project work where teams huddle in conference rooms looking for ways to solve the challenge. The dynamic is very similar but typically more animated and loud. The process takes time, and the results are typically not above par because of the limited creativity, but the process is there. Teamwork is an area with enough potential that it should be exploited once we can trigger the creativity bug.

III - Positive attitude

The power of good attitude in an employee is second only to his desire to learn. Being positive and engaged brings with it a tremendous amount of energy that spreads throughout the office. Here, it is difficult to find a person with a bad attitude or one not willing to join the team and work with a positive frame of mind. In the West, I have experienced how infectious a bad attitude can be. This will spread like the flu and is very hard to get out once it is in. The Chinese who I have worked with seldom show an unwillingness to try something new or to take on a bigger workload. I think this attitude is there from early on in life where parents will not accept failure and failure is much more likely if you have a negative attitude. The team dynamic also drives a positive environment and is often self-sustaining, regardless of the leadership influence.

I experienced a very rare case in China where the supervisor was a complete disappointment to me and his employees. His propensity to make the work seem arduous and overwhelming was quite disappointing. One would expect this to rub off on his employees and pretty quickly the entire group would be a mass of negativity and low morale. This was my experience in the U.S.. The supervisor sets the tone and the group follows. The U.S. employees also naturally gravitate toward the bad attitude. They love it when there is a valid reason to moan and groan. Even if there is just a small feeling of negativity in the room, they will feed on it until everyone is consumed by it. But in China, the situation I described never leads to a distraught group. Somehow they see right through the supervisor, tag him as ineffective in his ability to teach them anything because of his bad attitude, and they move on. They find whatever small hope they can to feed on and turn the group into a strong sub-organization underneath him where he becomes irrelevant and ignored. This suits him, as he is inherently lazy and is happy to sit by while his group moves around him and makes the world go round. Needless to say that this response from the group, as commendable as it is, has created a shield around him and he is protected from exposure. So, as you can imagine, it takes a while for us to recognize the issue and remove him from the organization. In this situation, where typically the boss drives everything, the need to learn and succeed is the stronger need and leads to a solution. The group finds a way to heal around him like scar tissue surrounds a foreign object, isolating it from the body. They continue to lead themselves and achieve success.

The positive attitude and how it penetrates the organization creates an environment that is not only inspiring to work in but truly unique to the Chinese.

IV - Executers

For every company there is a set of work that is routine and boring. It is repetitive and mundane, but it is necessary. Typical factory work in South China, where the Apple products are made or plastic dolls are dressed and packaged, is what most people will think about when we talk about repetitive jobs. There are millions of people doing these jobs in thousands of factories around the country. The cost of manual labor is still low enough to resist the automation of these processes.

However, my focus is on the routine processes in an office environment where we are working with degreed people in areas that require a level of computer expertise and undergraduate knowledge. A typical space that fits this is the Shared Services area where companies are building centers to manage procurement, logistics, accounting, and help desks for their global companies. The driver behind large Shared Service Centers is twofold. Firstly, it is of interest to executives because of the labor arbitrage that can be gained by moving work out of a high-pay country like Singapore or Germany into a low-cost country like

India or the Philippines. Secondly, it is an attractive option to force standardization of global processes by putting them under one roof and management. This standardization brings value in itself as the variants of processes become fewer and the work involved in propping up these variants and holding their hands throughout the process becomes less and less. It instills a level of discipline in the rest of the organization who rely on the Shared Service Center to service them. They are forced to feed information into the center a certain way and expect it to come out a certain way.

India is probably your first thought when thinking about shared service or outsourced centers. You picture thousands of Indians sitting in cubicles answering telephone calls from around the world. The high-tech sector went to India because of the IT expertise and their ability to speak English. The model clearly works in the way it was intended and has created the level of frustration that is only just acceptable enough so as not to force companies to pull the plug and bring the jobs back home. The Philippines, who seem to command the lower wage rate in this level of employee, is an attractive country for more finance or insurance-type back office processing. Then, of course, there is Malaysia that offers, at a higher cost, a more stable economy and political environment at the moment, which some companies see as a good compromise.

Singapore was the only safe gateway to Asia fifteen years ago. Their British influence has secured English as a prominent business language. This language is referred to as *Singlish*, but when pushed, the Singaporeans are quite capable of talking the Queen's English. In addition, their modern infrastructure, business practices and tight control over fraud and common crime made this a safe and attractive place to put a regional headquarters. These regional headquarters grew as Asia did, and many companies found that their people were in Singapore but that their factories and customers were in Thailand, Indonesia, or China. As these factories grew and the executives and managers traveled into these countries more and more, the comfort level with doing business there improved. Then along came China, with such force and determination to become an economy to be reckoned with that Singapore started to feel the threat. Singapore has always held the status of the financial "Capital" of Asia, but once Beijing announced that it was positioning Shanghai to replace Singapore, and to replace Hong Kong for that matter, the world started to change.

Companies started to go where the customer base was, and once they started to realize the huge labor arbitrage between Singapore and China, things began to move quite quickly. Singapore was suddenly seen as a very expensive place to run a business. It was being compared to putting your headquarters in New York City. The advantages were not big enough to warrant the cost of being there. Over the last few years, the labor cost of a collage graduate was seven to ten times higher in Singapore than in a China.

So, step by step, the banks and related financial support companies set up shop in Shanghai and closed down, or at least scaled back, their Singapore organizations. Manufacturing corporations followed suit into Shanghai and then ultimately moved lower value jobs into Tier II cities more westward. These so-called Tier II cities are designated by Beijing and carry this awful burden of not being quite up to scratch when compared to the Tier I cities such as Beijing and Shanghai. There are specific measurements behind the designation, such as income per capita and population size. Nonetheless, the Tier II cities had the advantage of keeping their salaries much lower than the Tier 1 cities, and thus they attracted the slightly lower value work supporting the manufacturing sector. Some of these cities took the initiative and became Shared Service cities. A small city called Chengdu, that plays home to more than twelve million people, played this card very well.

"Build it and they will come."

This is the approach that Chengdu took when setting themselves up as a Shared Service city with the right wage rate. They designated a huge area of land on the outskirts of their city as the high-tech zone. They intended to attract high-tech companies to bring the help desks, support centers, and R&D groups to Chengdu. They wanted to be the Shared Service Center of the country and region. They invested massive amounts of cash and built not only office buildings to house these companies they hoped to attract but also employee housing inside the designated area. The intent was to offer affordable housing to attract the right talent from around the country to support the job creation that would follow these companies. They set up Shared Service conferences, which included tours around the zone, and wined and dined the executives of the companies on their list. The right tax incentives were offered, and infrastructure was not only promised but already built and waiting for them. The economic development department of the Chengdu Government employed slick English speaking advocates to be able to communicate with Expats and visiting executives. International schools and executive housing was put on display to ensure that management would be personally attracted to the city. The outlay up front must have taken obscene amounts of money, but most impressive of all was the absolute audacity of the government that this approach would work. And it did. Hundreds of brand name corporations, such as Motorola, Intel, and SAP, have significant organizations in Chengdu now. They are supporting China and the Asia region with a move toward becoming global support centers.

The audacity of the Chinese Government to assume that they can start to play in the regional space of Shared Service Centers is quite understandable if you believe that they see what I see. Simply put, the Chinese have been conditioned right through their education to execute flawlessly. Their learning is centered on repetition of Chinese characters, math problems, and the spoken word. The education process spoonfeeds the children and requires them to regurgitate the same answer over and over. If we see their lack of creativity as a weakness, then their ability to execute repetitive tasks with perfect precision is a great strength in a Shared Service Center world. Shared Service Centers are built to process similar transactions or processes from around the world as efficiently and effectively as possible. That means accurate and cheap. These are considered low-value areas of work that should be moved to low-cost regions of the world where they support the basic processes of a large corporation.

My experience when measuring efficiency between a similar Chinese group, an American group, and a European group was quite an eye opener for the Western crowd. Three groups were processing the same type of work and were measured on speed and accuracy. We used individual time-tracking measures, and errors were logged along the way. We did this for a few months and then analyzed the data. In terms of the efficiency metric, which measured how many employees were needed to process an equal amount of work each month, we found the American and European team to be equal. This made these two teams feel pretty good about their efficiency metric, until we showed them the Chinese numbers. It was unbelievable to me at first, and I think still to this day a little unbelievable to the Western groups, but we found that the Chinese required 40% less people to do the same work. This measure was based on a work day that could extend into the night if needed, which we didn't measure. So, the first thought was that the Chinese were working a lot of overtime to achieve this amount of work with so few people. When we had the overtime data compiled, we discovered that actually the American team was doing way more overtime than the other teams. Then came the Europeans and finally the Chinese with limited overtime. To make the disparity even more obvious, I looked deeper into the overtime in China and found that the teamwork aspect kicks in during after work hours. In critical periods of the month, the whole team will remain at work until all teammates have completed their tasks. This group support had actually made the real overtime numbers seem higher than they really were in China.

Efficiency is only one side of the coin. It is of no value if the effectiveness is weak. You can be very quick at what you do, but if you are making mistakes all the time, then the speed doesn't really count for much. So we looked at the accuracy of the Chinese team compared to the others. Much to the disappointment of the American team, we found that the error rate in China was significantly lower than that of the other teams. There were some factors at play in this, related to the complexity in America, but overall, there was no doubt that this Chinese team had set the bar very high.

As we talked about possible reasons for this Chinese ability to be this efficient and effective, it became pretty clear to me that the ability to *execute* quickly and flawlessly was the key driver. It wasn't a result of excessive training, overqualified employees, or simple processes. It was because of a natural ability to generate results through a commitment to perfection.

V - The power of the relationship

The final strength that is so important to the efficiency of working in China is the power of the relationship. If you have worked or done business in China, you may be wondering why I see this as a strength. One might argue that the relationship aspect of doing business is very burdensome and certainly slows down the process of reaching an agreement or moving forward on a negotiation. Agreements are only made once a personal relationship has developed and a certain level of trust is reached. This is quite typical in all of Asia. I also found this to be very frustrating at first, until I realized the motivation behind this.

i. The weakness of the contract

A lot of business arrangements are based on trust and not on a contract. The U.S. is probably the extreme opposite, where contracts rule and the relationship with your business partner is not half as important as the relationship with your lawyer.

To give you a sense of how strong the contract is in China, let me tell you a true story. A group of us met with a very large Chinese bank to finalize and sign a loan agreement. We had been through this loan process before, so the meeting was expected to be simple and straightforward. But when we had almost concluded the final document review, the bank passed along a new contract supplement and explained that the Chinese Government now required certain restrictions to be included in the contract. These clauses seemed to be adding some form of control to what they called "Hot Lending".

Hot lending described the black market for commercial loans. Beijing likes to know what is going on in their economy, and owning the major banks and controlling the flow of money was paramount to either keeping inflation in check or being able to heat up the economy as needed. Hot money was a market for cash-rich Chinese to lend to other local entrepreneurs without the formality of the banking structure. There is much cash in a few Chinese's hands, and they don't know what to do with it. Some of this cash is off the books, so banking it was not a good option. The real estate bubble was worrying some investors and the stock market was not as attractive anymore, so this cash made it onto the black money market for high-yield loans to those who wanted to expand their companies.

When Hot money became a booming business, Beijing lost part of its ability to manage the economy by raising bank interest rates because this Hot money flowed freely outside of their control.

So when this contract supplement was passed across the table, we huddled around it, and with good Western contract culture imbedded in our brains, we started asking line by line questions so we could fully understand what we were chopping (signing). After asking the third question and being met with the third round of blank expressions, I began to wonder why this large bank was unable to answer the questions we had. Surely other clients had already been through this process with them and we weren't the first company to have all these questions, so I asked. The answer they gave us was that all of their other clients had simply signed the document without question. They had borrowed millions of Chinese Yuan without fully understanding the legal ramifications for doing so. How could this be? We were dealing with one of the top three banks in the country, and their clients were all significant corporations.

As it turned out, the contract was not important to the Chinese companies. Signing the contract is as simple as checking the interest rate and the repayment period and moving on to the good stuff, which is getting the money. Years earlier, over many meals and many bottles of wine, the bank's other clients had reached an agreement to do business. There was mutual trust, and the contract was only paper. Any contract dispute down the road was exactly that — down the road. It is understood by both parties that the value of the contract is merely a solid starting point for negotiating an agreement. The relationship was a much stronger contract than any piece of paper. This paper was a clear way to write down the basic information of the agreement, but it didn't really mean anything more than that.

In a dispute, there are no lawyers negotiating a settlement. There are old friends yelling at each other over a large round dinner table until the rice wine settles the yelling into a slow rumble and finally a happy back-slapping agreement is reached. He who holds his drink better comes out stronger in the settlement. The contract is not nearly as important as the relationship with the other party.

ii Dealing with a dispute

In the U.S., lawyers are a key component to doing business. Contract disputes are all too easily moved to the legal stage, as there is no foundation to work from if there is a disagreement. There is no personal relationship between the two parties to allow a starting point for friendly discussions. The business relationships are short term and often designed for maximum immediate benefit for both parties. Even if there is a long-term contract, by the time there is a dispute both sides have turned over their staff so many times that no one knows each other. In the Wild West, everyone carried a gun on their hip to help resolve *disputes*. Now days, everyone carries a cell phone on their hip with their lawyer's number on speed dial.

In China, lawyers and judges are rarely used in a contract dispute. Traffic accidents, for example, are settled at the scene by the police officer. He is the judge and the jury at the scene. Cash changes hands in a settlement right there and then, and everyone goes home happy or unhappy, but it is over. There are no lawsuits, no lawyers, and no judges.

I know what you are thinking. *Who made the police officer "God"?* Well, the government did, and to be fair, he is in a much better situation to apply good judgment than a judge ten weeks later at a hearing. He can see the damage firsthand, talk to witnesses real time, and he doesn't have to listen to a couple of ego-driven lawyers who have twisted the truth until the truth itself is screaming for forgiveness. The police officer has complete power, and from a few cases of personal experience, they seem to be very fair and resolute.

The one downfall to this immediate on-the-site ruling is that the people involved in the accident, for example, have quickly learned that they need to be their own lawyer. They need to dramatize their case to make their side of the argument seem stronger. This is typically achieved through theatrics.

Wang Hu was driving along the road when all of a sudden Li Ping pulled out right in front of him on her electric scooter. She was on her cell phone with her friend who would be buying her handbag in New York for her. She was so excited about this that she didn't realize the car was right there. She hit the brakes, but the car tapped her back wheel and she fell over into the street.
Wang Hu hit the brakes hard and felt a sickening feeling in his stomach as he saw her fall over. He knew instinctively that she was not hurt, but he knew this would hurt his wallet. As soon as he stopped the car and opened the door, he heard the screaming. Based on the screams coming from the other side of the road, clearly

he must have parked his car on her leg or something. Everyone had stopped and was looking on with disdain. He ran around the car and saw that she was lying on her back six feet away from his car. The scooter had fallen over into the road and she was lying next to it. He ran over and asked her if she was okay, but she was inconsolable. He was convinced that she had suffered multiple fractures, but really there was nothing wrong with her.

When Li Ping had first felt the tap on her back wheel, she had lost her balance and stepped off the scooter as it fell on the ground. She stumbled briefly and then in an instant understood that she needed to fall down. The dilemma of finding money for that new handbag had just resolved itself. She fell on her back and looked up at the car, hoping it was imported. The more expensive the car, the more likely the driver had money. She saw the Buick emblem on the front and started to scream. No one came running; no one offered to help her up. She would have refused had they tried, because it was important for the accident scene to look as impressive as possible when the police officer arrived. She bent her leg under her in an awkward way and reached over for her cell phone that had dropped from her hand as she'd fallen. Dialing the police was step one in the process that would take an hour to resolve.

The police officer arrived, and Li Ping's moaning intensified as she tried to make the accident look a lot worse that it was. She was hoping that her scooter had incurred some damage, at least enough to justify a little extra toward her compensation. The car had a small scratch, and Wang Hu was obviously fine. The officer walked over to Li Ping and took her account of the event. She embellished it as much as she could while trying to charm the officer a little. Wang Hu told his account, and a few witnesses were asked to contribute. Those who were sympathetic to the lady on the ground recounted the horror, and others simply laughed and explained what was going on.

There was no ambulance needed and no tow-truck, so the officer made an offer to the parties individually. Wang Hu would have to pay for the scooter repairs, two hundred Yuan, and settle for Li Ping's pain and suffering of seven hundred Yuan. Wang Hu protested loudly and explained that it wasn't even his fault, but Li Ping's bent leg and scooter on the ground left his story pretty weak. So, in the end, he handed over the cash and settled the claim. The police office wrote out an official receipt and exchanged the cash with Li Ping. Li Ping stood up, brushed herself off, picked up her scooter, and drove off. Wang Hu kicked his front tire in frustration, got back in his car, and continued off to work.

In these situations, the police officer has complete control, and even if you try to disagree with him, he will eventually convince you to accept his ruling and move on. If you are brave enough, you have the right to take down his badge number and report the situation at the police station; however, unless you have blatant proof that you have been wronged at the scene, don't bother.

In another case, a vendor came to the office to dispute a short payment we had made to him. We tried to reason with him and explain the logic for the short payment, but he was adamant that we were cheating him. Suddenly, he got up and stormed out of the office. Twenty minutes later, he arrived at the reception area with a police officer. If I had been brand-new in China, I might have quickly written a check to make the problem go away, but I wasn't, so we sat down with the officer and went through the case in detail. After listening for a while, it became clear to the policeman that the vendor was living in his own world and needed to be set straight. The vendor sensed that he was losing the argument and the discussion got very heated. He started banging on the table and shouting for his rights. The officer explained that his rights had reached an end and roughly walked him out of the building, threatening to put him in jail if he returned to harass us. Case closed.

If you have ever lived through a long, drawn-out legal case in the U.S., you can't help but appreciate the swiftness of the Chinese system. The lawyers and judges are left alone to focus on the big issues facing the country. They are working on large cases of corruption or embezzlement where people are jailed or executed. Their time is spent making sure those serious criminals are punished adequately.

iii Building the relationship

So if we agree that the contract carries little importance and that disputes are handled efficiently in real time, you start to understand why relationships are so important in business. Fighting a dispute is much less desirable than avoiding a dispute altogether by doing business with people who you trust and with whom you have a longstanding relationship. The core of a Chinese relationship is trust, and it is vital for Chinese society and business. Paper-based trust in the form of a contract and a tough lawyer doesn't apply in China. They have to rely on the relationship and the underlying trust to ensure smooth deals and continued business.

The power of the relationship is quite significant. It takes a long time to develop, but once it exists and there is mutual respect and trust, the bond is seldom broken. The typical business relationship is built up over many dinners and a lot of Baijiu, a clear drink made from sorghum grain or rice and carries a punch that hits you twice, once when you drink it in the evening and again the next day when it seeps from your pores and you smell it all day. It is served from a beautiful blue bottle into a small glass jug that sits in front of your dinner plate. Your small jug is used to fill up your shot glass as you need it, which is often. The problem with the small jug is that you don't notice that it is constantly being refilled by the waitress. Many times I have tried to keep count of how many shots I have had based on how many times I emptied the jug, but with the perpetually-full little jug, my counting often faded into an incoherent chuckle as the table seemed to be spinning along with the guests.

The ritual of a dinner and the *drinking game* need only be experienced once to teach you that unless you get better at the game, you should politely refuse the next invitation. Dinner typically starts at 6:00 P.M. and ends at 8:00 P.M. sharp. That is the good news. The time is defined, and the ability to predict the end allows you to pace yourself. Two hours is very short, and it is surprising how drunk you can get in this short time frame. After all, you are drinking shots of 80% to 120% proof, which amount to around 40% to 60% alcohol volume.

A business dinner goes something like this: After normal the meet and greet and general chatting, you sit around this large table with a huge Lazy Susan in the middle. No, this isn't a girl called Susan; it is a big circle of glass that spins in the center of the table. This allows the shared dishes to be rotated from guest to guest. The seating is prearranged for the senior members of the party, who typically sit next to each other at the back of the room facing the door. The rest of the group gently negotiates and insists on where everyone should sit. The closer you sit to the host and senior guest implies the more senior you are. Giving up your closer seat to your counterpart from the other company is seen as a sign of respect for them and a generous offer. The first dish arrives and everyone stares at it, waiting for the host to invite his guest, which was often me, to take the first helping. As they wait, the discussion about what we should drink ensues. The choices are always between beer, red wine, and white wine. To me, white wine sounded pretty good the first time I was offered it, and I made my mistake in selecting it. I was hoping for a good chardonnay, but out came the *Baijiu*, much to the delight of my host.

To start the meal, the first bite is a trepid moment for me as I use my chopsticks to try and pick up the least slippery looking items on the table. Everyone watches with interest to see a foreigner manage chop sticks, and then they hastily dig in once my chopsticks have reached my mouth. This step is quickly followed by the drinking. The host will toast his counterpart, and one by one the little shot glasses are drunk and the little clear jugs are filled. The mood quickly moves from fun to hilarious. Everyone around the table feels the need to toast you with the evil words, "Gam bei," which implies bottoms up, and you begin to absorb this powerful liquid into your bloodstream. During the meal, you try to eat as much as possible to dilute the effect, but how much can you really eat if you have to use little sticks to pick everything up? So you resort to the drinking game to try and slow down the pace of abuse to your body. When the next person tries to toast you, you protest with a smile that their glass is not full enough and gleefully pour some out of yours into theirs. Or you reach across to retrieve your little devil jug and promptly top up their glass. This debate over who has enough or not enough is a fun tactic to delay the amount you drink. Within a two hour drinking window, you can delay quite a bit.

You can also strategically align your side of the table to gang up on your host and have him toast with each one of them individually. If this is done right, you can knock him out of the game early. But he is typically well versed in this game and has his professional drinker with him to keep you on your heels by relentlessly saying, "Gam bei." The professional drinkers, as they are affectionately known, are used as a decoy for their boss and are employed as admin assistants, translators, or public affairs people, and they have this unique skill of being able to absorb huge amounts of alcohol. The very good ones are able to supplement their boss' Baijiu for a watered-down version without anyone noticing. The surprising fact about these professional drinkers is that they are invariably women, and small women to boot! You know, the petite Chinese ladies who you could mistake for a child from a distance. Yes, those little ladies can somehow drink you under the table and save your counterpart from a sever hangover all at the same time.

Finally, after two hours of the game, your friendship with your host has improved dramatically through mutual respect for being able to drink the good stuff. You have built a solid foundation for a future relationship, with a clear understanding that many more such nights will be needed to fully cement the relationship. And, all of a sudden, the watermelon arrives. Yes, for any foreigner, the sight of the watermelon is a glorious one. It signals that the evening has ended, that the drinking has stopped, and after a quick bite of watermelon, you are shaking hands, bowing, and leaving the room to go home. The two-hour dinner, ending with such precision, is the key to being able to drink inexplicable quantities of this white wine and still be standing at eight o'clock. The secret is that you can factor in the final twenty minutes it takes for the effect to kick in. What you consume in those last twenty minutes is only felt after you leave the room and stagger into the waiting car. Your driver and then your family at home get to see the full effects of the event, and if you have teenagers like I do, they tend to quietly video your homecoming. But your host has only seen your impressive ability to drink as well as he can.

Relationships are formed in many different ways, and not only through excess situations such as the one I just described. They are built over time outside of work by playing sports together, or eating and shopping together. The effort, if you will, is significant, but the rewards are great.

In an office environment, the relationship factor between peers and teams is where we see another aspect of the relationship power. Office culture can go two ways. It can become a hostile environment where people stick to themselves and fight to keep work from seeping into their little cubicle. I have worked in environments that remind me of a girls high school where little cliques exist and they gossip about other cliques. The culture becomes one of blaming and pointing the finger.

Collaboration to solve issues or develop solutions becomes more of an exercise to protect territory from losing work or to prevent attracting more work. Using tools like Lean Sigma, where a facilitator manages the room, tends to be the only effective way to get these people working together. In this toxic environment, when a process breaks down, it is patched up with duct tape and sent down to the next work station. The next person either avoids eye contact with the problem and passes it along, or they rip the duct tape off to expose a nemesis next door. These environments tend to spin off the good people who want more out of a job than this and leave behind the ones who enjoy this type of work culture. These bottom feeders of the corporation are intent on ensuring that nothing gets done without a complaint or a complication. Every new idea that is raised is attacked like a virus by these people who focus on what is wrong with the idea and why it can't be achieved. They have an amazing ability to foresee the areas of concern versus areas of opportunity. Once this culture has taken over the group, as newcomers are hired they very quickly follow the mob and adapt their attitude to fit in with the rest. Most Western people seem to easily gravitate toward complaining versus driving positive thoughts and actions. And once this culture has taken hold, it takes a huge effort to change it. It can only be achieved if the bad apples are taken out of the organization and the followers are strongly advised not to fill the void left by the bad apples. Secondly, they are given positive role models and team leaders to follow. Even after this, it takes a lot of continuous cheerleading and positive reinforcement to ensure that the new culture takes hold lower in the organization. Even when you think it is taking hold, you can still find pockets of naysayers privately bashing those trying to be positive.

In China, there is a natural sense of positive attitude and motivation. There is also a great sense of teamwork to hold the groups together. The culture already has a good foundation to work from. Taking this foundation and building up an environment and culture that is unshakably positive and is driven requires leveraging the power of the relationship. With some time, effort, and money, a company can facilitate the forming of these relationships and the speed at which they form. Simple things, such as team-building outings, office sports teams, celebration dinners, and various cross-functional competitions are ideas that can accelerate the forming of new friendships in the group. It still takes time, but the benefit we see once this group strength is built is significant compared to the initial outlay. It also sets up the culture for life, which absorbs new hires into it and ensures that the positive culture is perpetual.

Summary: What we have to work with

What more could any country ask for from its population than to be positive and motivated? Add in their yearning to learn throughout their lives, staying motivated and driven to execute flawlessly in an environment where trust and relationships are paramount to a healthy society. China has those qualities that a young U.S. might have had, where the American Dream was out there waiting for anyone motivated enough to go and live it.

However, we must not forget when considering China's ability to move into the global arena that there are many gaps and challenges to overcome. These gaps are huge, and their country runs in such a different way to the West that it is hard to imagine this country ever reaching its full potential. Short-time visitors and potential investors in China often walk away shaking their heads, preferring to let the Chinese live in their Chinese world. Others grit their teeth and invest because everyone else is, and not doing so would put them behind their peers. China and its business culture is not for the weak or sensitive by any means; it is a daily challenge to operate under their rules, so being able to manage their own companies in our world is not regarded as a real threat to the West.

However, when you look at their amazing qualities and compare them to what you see in people in the West now, you can start to see how this population and this country really could get there and eclipse the U.S. as the world's number one superpower. They have the ability to learn much quicker than young Westerners, and they have the drive and motivation to do it, given the right tools.

TAKING ON THE MANAGEMENT GAP CHALLENGE

The challenge the Chinese have to face is not within their own country. They have more than enough strength in business matters to build up their domestic economy. Where they will fall short is when they outgrow their own economy and really want to be a world superpower, driving other economies with their own needs. They will need to invest in other countries and run these corporations around the world, just like the Western companies are investing in China today.

Today, as these Western companies invest and try to run their subsidiaries in China, they are confronted with a serious problem. What they are faced with is a new playing field — the Chinese playing field, where the rules are different and the ball is not round. Actually, there is no ball at all. It is more of an invisible ball that is passed around between good friends. If you want to play, then you need to make friends and adapt to their rules. Trying to apply U.S. rules in a Chinese business process is like trying to put a square peg in a round hole. This same problem will occur when the Chinese start to expand their companies abroad and send their own expatriates over to run them. They will not succeed if they are playing the wrong game.

In the first section, I talk about the gaps that are evident in the Chinese work style and skill set. These gaps or challenges will hold them back from playing on the international playing field. We have seen that they are quite adept at playing in China, and with the help of a managed economy, they have shown the world that they can really produce the results of which every emerging country dreams. However, these gaps will hold them back from stepping out of China and playing with the big kids in the world playground. The rules and expectations are different, and if China wants to develop to their full global potential, be running huge corporations in the U.S. or Europe, and be competing on their soil under their rules, then they need some help in learning to play a little differently.
The good news is that there is such a wealth of positive attributes in place inside this culture that it is quite possible to leverage these as tools to close these gaps and prepare them for the big league.

I - Understanding the motivators

As you embark on the challenge to bring a group of people in a company to the point where they are able to play in the global playing field, you need to start with a clear understanding of the motivators. Many foreign managers assume that their motivators are universal and should work anywhere. For example, the assumption that employees will buy into a vision just because the CEO wrote it down is a dangerous one. The average educated Chinese employee will need much more than that to buy into it. Just because they are taught to follow and not lead does not mean they will follow blindly. Many managers have issued the command to follow only to find that he has lost his troop half a mile down the road because he has not explained *why* they should follow.

Remember that the primary motivator in this environment is, "What's in it for me?" As explained earlier, this should not be seen as a selfish or self-centered attitude, but merely one of self-preservation in a world with so many others to compete against. It is also the motivator that stems from the huge economic and social pressure on them as they run through their careers looking for the quickest way to reach a level of financial security. Their financial security will ensure good schools for their children and financial stability in their retirement. Wasting time by following someone down a road that may be dead end cannot be risked. The time wasted would allow their peers to move ahead of them in the race for success, and hence the question, "What's in it for me?"

II - Communicating the Vision

The vision needs to be a carefully planned document, built in a slightly different way to what would be conventional in the West. The vision should be exactly that, a look-see at the future. The picture of the future needs to be drawn with enough detail and explanation to help your employees decide if the journey down this road is worth their time and effort. The vision must attract them to this place by appealing to their motivators.

The place you want to take them needs to be a place where the primary problems are solved. This should include improving creativity, significantly improving retention and the long-term stability of the group, and providing competent leadership with the ability to lead and grow the organization. The tools and transport you should use to move your organization along the road toward this place should fully leverage the strengths of the group, such as their eagerness to learn, positive attitude, teamwork, and the power of their relationships. In the most efficient way you can imagine, you should also use their innate ability to execute.

If done right, the journey will be challenging but possible. This will appeal to their need to learn something new. Having them work with natural tools, such as relationships and teams, will help them accept the challenge. The place you are taking them must appeal to their most basic motivator so they can see how they will benefit from the end state. Watch carefully in the group for those who are the brightest, who catch on and see the vision clearly and the value it offers. Use those people to help sell the idea to others and in their own unwritten social code translate the value into a recognizable format. The decision to climb aboard is individual, and you will not see a sheep-like approach when it comes to these important decisions. Each person will make up his own mind, so don't expect that once you have the majority on board that the group pressure will bring the rest along. Each person perceives value differently because their own needs are different, and ensuring that the value is shown in a lot of different ways can help to catch the attention of the few stragglers who can't seem to find a good reason to buy in.

Similar to the West, the goal is to have them make the process or journey become their own. This goal is defined the same way, but the method of getting there is a little different. However, once you have the ownership and commitment to start the journey, you can feel comfortable that you won't lose anyone along the way, as the team effect will kick in once you leave. The team effect ensures a cohesive unit of dedication and drives the process forward to a final result that will meet and more than likely exceed your expectations.

III - Solving the retention problem

The first step of the journey must be to solve the retention problem. Second only to a sick corporate culture, retention is the most important area on which to focus.

I put retention ahead of the culture because this journey will help heal and define a new company culture for you. There is no one specific action that determines a culture; it is a process with many inputs, where the whole is greater than the sum of its parts. The culture itself cannot be *created* by you; it can only be aided and supported. This journey will be the best you can do to help it germinate and grow into something strong.

High turnover and the inability to retain employees for long periods of time, which in China is defined as more than one year at the moment, will render your company weak. You will be in constant retraining and firefighting mode, and you will have no time to engage in value-added areas. The problem need not be explained in-depth, because you understand this from wherever you work in the world. But in China, the problem is severe and getting worse. So starting out your journey by focusing on improved productivity or grand ideas of new product launches will quite easily fail again and again until you can operate with a stable workforce.

There are seven areas I identify as retention drivers in China. However, before we start discussing solutions in these seven areas, a quick word on the approach. The U.S. often pays lip service to the K.I.S.S. principle. The principle is sound and makes all the difference to what you need to do. However, in my experience, this principle is ignored in the real solution-building because simple in the U.S. implies stupid. Stupid does not get us promoted or revered. Teams in the U.S. that are tasked to develop a solution invariably come back with an over-engineered and highly complex solution to an often simple problem. The cultural issue driving this over-worked result is that they work in a democratic system where everyone has to have his say. Decisions are formed based on consensus. Compromises are made to keep everyone in the team happy, and further compromises are made to keep their stakeholders happy. The result is messy, complex, and impractical. The team reports back to the executives with their product, standing together in the front of the conference room. They will walk you through the seven steps to being able to set up the nine steps to arrange a meeting to execute the next twelve steps in the process. The solutions are very academic and would look great in an MBA thesis — but not in the real world. The proud team hands over the process and walks away to begin developing another ridiculous solution to another simple problem. The new process owners take the eighty-five slide process, roll their eyes, and continue with what they were always doing. What they were always doing was probably pretty close to being good, because it has evolved out of a practical need to execute the process efficiently. All it really needed was a few tweaks, some automation, and a control plan.

So when I mention keeping these solutions simple, I really mean it, because any other way is a waste of time. And we know how the Chinese hate to waste time. Any solution that arrives back with bells and whistles or any fat on it needs to be trimmed before it is rolled out. We are not trying to win an award on ingenuity in these situations. We are trying to drive certain programs and processes through the organizations that get us the most bang for the buck.

i. On-Boarding

The first area identified as a retention driver is on-boarding. On-boarding starts right after the offer is made to a new employee and they accept the offer to join your company. That time between the offer letter and the first month on board is critical to setting the right frame of mind for the new employee. You have heard of buyer's remorse; well, there is also a sense of *hiring remorse* with people who have just resigned and the thrill of job seeking has gone and they are waiting out their notice period. They are amongst old friends, while their current boss is still leveraging his relationship with them, and they are beginning to dread the thought of starting again. That full month is a lonely time, and this *hiring remorse* can be fatal if not dealt with.

Step one is to immediately assign a buddy to the new hire after they accept the offer. Have the buddy meet with the new hire inside that notice period, perhaps for lunch a couple of times to talk about the company. Having the buddy take a few colleagues with him would be good advice as well. Friendships (relationships) are extremely powerful, and starting this bonding early pays back well. The manager should also be emailing periodically to keep in touch and offer words of encouragement and excitement.

Day one is made easier by knowing someone in the office; however, this is always a high-stress situation. The key to day one is to keep them busy. Leaving them at a desk without a user ID, PC, or something to do is awkward and depressing. Make sure there is printed literature, policies, and company information on their desk to at least help them give the impression of being busy. Being prepared for the arrival is also important. Simple things, such as having the computer and Internet access ready goes a long way toward helping them feel valuable. One simple idea is to produce a road map that outlines the steps they will take over the first few weeks and also highlights specific policies and contacts. This roadmap shows specific steps they need to take, for example, meeting with HR or taking safety training, steps that each new employee needs to take and at what date. This gives them an immediate action plan for the short term. This roadmap also gives them an introduction to those policies and procedures that they can self-study about travel expense claims or emergency evacuations. And finally, it would include a concise list of key contacts in the building or globally that they might need if they need help with anything. This list can help them help themselves and avoid having to bug their buddies or peers all the time. It creates a certain sense of independence immediately.

The goal of on-boarding is to integrate the new hire as quickly as possible and have them adding value as soon as possible. So once they are in the building and the logistics are taken care of, education is the focus. The Chinese are quick learners and can educate themselves much more efficiently than their average Western counterparts. The Western approach involves a lot of watching and learning from the outgoing employee, if you are lucky enough to even have a hand-over period. The Chinese approach is more about giving them the desk procedures, the system training, and the control points for them to study. There is some teaching involved, but only to the point where the tools are taught. The process can be read and understood by themselves. Their ability to come up to speed quickly is quite phenomenal. They definitely seem to have something to prove, but more than that, there is a certain pride in what they can do and the need to show their manager what they are made of.

On-board them well, and you have a dedicated employee from day one who will attach himself to the organization and continue to support and enhance the culture you are developing. Proper on-boarding also avoids a false start. A false start is when a new hire arrives on day one already looking for another job. They never engage and simply cause you to waste another eight weeks refilling the position. This is when you lose the hand-over period and start to stress the existing organization. This work stress can be toxic to the culture.

It is that simple: Assign a buddy to make contact in the remorse period. Build a roadmap to take them through the first few weeks. Give them the tools to learn the job and shine. Implementing and managing a program like this is simple and sustainable.

i Career Plan

Career planning as a term was foreign, literally, to everyone who I first worked with in China. Careers were decided in high school, if not earlier. The initial selection is between private or public sector. Government jobs are still highly sought after as they allow you to carry great power in the community and in your job. The government has always set very difficult entrance exams that are quite famous for attracting hundreds of thousands more applicants than make the grade. This tradition goes back hundreds of years. Family support can also buy you a spot through their strong political relationships. Second focus choice, assuming that you chose the private sector, is between math/science and language. From there, a language university, an engineering university, or a math and accounting university is chosen. After graduation and arriving in their first job, they typically hand over their career to the manager and hope for the best. Sadly though, their career normally ends up in the bottom drawer as the manager has no sense of the art of career management.

This topic is critical in China and has to be addressed if they have any hope in developing the global players they will need.

The first message that needs to be delivered on careers is that the employee owns his own career. It doesn't belong to the boss nor should it be left to fate. It has to be planned, worked, and adjusted periodically. Getting this message across is so important, because without this realization and eventual responsibility, the next steps of how to manage their career will be futile.

The Chinese mind is much better at logical thinking than it is at conceptual thinking. Career planning is unfortunately mostly conceptual. It's almost as difficult as strategic thinking because it is looking forward into the unknown without much certainty that this can be achieved. As a general rule when dealing in areas requiring conceptual thinking, revert to diagrams. Looking at a picture and discussing something conceptual allows the logical side of the brain to get involved, and this helps the process. What I found to be very successful is drawing up the organizational chart within each functional area, taking out the names, and limiting each type of job to one box. For example, if you have twelve buyers, then one box named *buyers* would suffice. If there is a distinction between those twelve buyers of products being bought and these differ in difficulty and allow for knowledge growth along their career path, then keep separate boxes for these. Each of these jobs should be placed in vertical and horizontal progression. What this means is that the obvious career path would always point upwards. But promotional steps vertically are not always possible in a short amount of time. So make sure the possible career moves allow for horizontal moves that are seen as growth moves to help broaden their knowledge. Keep in mind that although promotion and money is an important motivator for the Chinese, the need to be learning something new is equally motivating. So the vertical progression is not always needed at each step of the way.

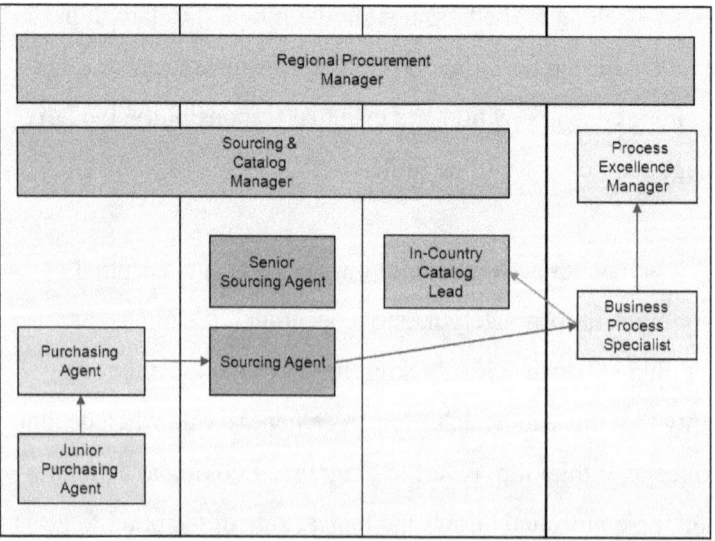

Have them draw lines on the diagram from where they are now through some logical career steps. Note that the Business Process Specialist role in this diagram is shown slightly elevated compared to the Sourcing Agent role. It is likely that these roles are at the same salary band level, but in the eyes of management and the employees, this is seen as a superior role because of its specialized knowledge and skill. It is important to understand what jobs are seen as more complex or more important than others in order to get the vertical alignment right. Don't make the mistake of showing a diagram to someone who is then shocked to see their role depicted as a lesser role than what is commonly accepted. These visual effects with horizontal opportunities will help them buy into a slower vertical progression, which is more realistic.

Career planning must be done alongside someone who is competent and can give advice on what is realistic and what is not. One aspect that is different in China is timing. Typically, Western companies expect two to three years in one job before you are allowed to apply for another position. This allows twelve to eighteen months to climb the learning curve and another year or so to improve the role and add value to the company. In China, the learning curve typically takes six to nine months, and then perfection is reached quickly. Improvement and adding value are not as prominent as in the East unless you take measures to encourage and support it, but more on that later. So I think a typical job for an average Chinese employee with a degree should be between twelve and eighteen months. This quick turnaround has a significant impact on retention of your workforce, because you are constantly feeding that need to learn something new. These moves from job to job can be subtle in nature and may only be a shift of focus area from perhaps a domestic role to an export role, but as long as fifty percent of the job content changes, there is immediate learning, engagement, and satisfaction.

iii Training

Training can take many forms, but it is essential that you commit the resources and have a plan. The good news is that getting participants for training classes is not a problem in China. They will line up for free courses that will teach them something. The challenge of participation is more centered around making sure that the right people get signed up first.

Training or study of some nature is very natural, and the Chinese are at home in a lecture or study environment. Most of the young professionals I have been exposed to are also working on an advanced degree or certification regardless of their role in the company. Continuous learning is expected by their parents and by themselves. The courses that seem to be the most attractive are those that are more tactical and job-skill focused. The courses that are around soft skills, such as how to negotiate better or how to communicate more effectively, are less sought after. So there is a need to advertise the value in this soft skill training for those aspiring to be leaders in the company. Even at the younger age, training around organization and time management needs a little nudge. Courses with tests at the end are not popular in the U.S. and are even outlawed in some companies to avoid embarrassing the attendees. However, these young guys thrive on this and compete vigorously to achieve top marks.

Training programs should support the two basic areas of their jobs. Firstly, technical competencies need to be developed for their current role and for future roles. Once future roles have been identified in their career plan, it is a good idea to introduce the candidate to the technical training prior to or concurrent with the change in job. This will speed up the transition and accelerate the accuracy and efficiency they will bring. This requires a robust training department and schedule or an investment in on-line training courses, but it is well worth the investment once your processes are standardized and not changing too often.

Secondly, training of soft competencies is important. Soft competencies are areas that need to be identified in each employee's development plan and worked on. This area will be discussed in more depth below, but suffice to say that this includes skills such as how to be a change agent or how to be more decisive and challenging. Offering training to build up skills that they are not sure they need can be challenging, but making these skills mandatory to career advancement is a great motivator.

Offering and advertising a comprehensive training program in both technical and soft competencies will not only attract new hires to your company but will help retain them in the long run.

iv Compensations & Benefits

Retaining employees through compensation is a slippery slope in an emerging country. The need for *more* is on everyone's minds and is seen every day when the neighbor shows off his latest acquisition. Everyone's desire or expectation for more is outpacing the supply. Today's environment demands eight to ten percent pay raises each year. If you want to use pay to motivate a special employee to stay, then you have to be competing with the business across the road. And they are offering twenty to thirty percent more. Very quickly you will find yourself offering thirty to forty percent raises to retain someone, and this is not realistic or prudent. My point is that you cannot compete on pay alone. You have to offer something that your competitor isn't thinking about. Pay needs to be competitive and needs to keep pace with the market, mostly to help attract good talent, but nothing more than that.

Pay should also follow the salary band logic, and as people move up the ladder, they are paid according to what the market would pay them outside. This is an area where it is very tempting to continue with ten to twenty percent pay hikes as people are promoted. This approach will result in them being paid below market very quickly as their skills increase. This will get you into trouble quickly. In China, the pay differential between a three-year experienced person and a manager is around ten times. The table below shows the abnormally sharp rise in scale over time. The annual merit increase you would have to apply to a person who consistently climbs the ladder is vastly different from that in the U.S.

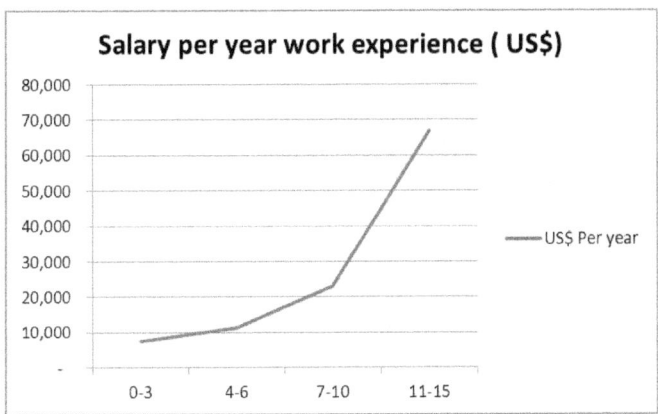

In order for you to take a good employee from an entry level university graduate junior, starting at five thousand U.S. dollars a year to a manager at sixty-eight thousand a year fifteen years later, you would need to give at least a 12.5% salary increase each year, over and above inflation of 8%-10%, just to keep them aligned with the market. This in itself is quite a task to manage, let alone trying to buy people to stay with your company.

So you have to focus on other benefits of your company and offer different reasons to stay. From what I have seen, people remain in a company based on a hierarchy of needs. These needs vary from person to person, but there seems to be a common theme that is worth exploring.

The three biggest reasons given by employees when asked why they remain at their company is:

1. Career development and opportunities
2. Working environment/company culture
3. Compensation and benefits

With compensation being difficult to manage, it is important to focus on the top two.

v Working Environment

The office community is a key area that factors into the working environment. Developing a community feeling where those key drivers such as relationships and teams come into play can really help keep people engaged in the company. The office community is built around simple ideas such as celebrating and decorating for various holidays or having daily stretching exercises in a conference room. It involves buying cakes for birthdays and posting photos of events on public boards. It can also reach out of the office by forming teams to play various sports, helping to fund them, and encouraging cheerleader groups from the office to support them as they compete with other companies or functions.

The Chinese love gifts. They also love photos and videos of themselves. Putting together workshops and communication meetings where there are simple prizes to give away and photos projected on the screen for them to make fun of each other makes for a good hour at the office. By simply facilitating the opportunity, it is impressive how quickly they are able to generate excitement and a sense of community.

Holidays must all be celebrated, and China has many fascinating festivals and holidays to leverage. They are also not shy about fully exploiting Christmas just to have a Christmas tree in the reception area with gifts for everyone. Valentine's day is big now, and we are also starting to see the Easter Bunny at the right time of the year. Each of these opportunities can be leveraged and enjoyed by all with very little effort.

As people play together like this, they form stronger relationships. Not only are these relationships formed within their own functions but also across functions. While helping retention, it also helps productivity as they start to work in cross-functional teams.

vi Work life balance

Work and life balance is very different in China compared to the U.S. In the States, people work long hours and then go home. Home life is typically very separate from work life. There is a clear line between work and home in terms of when one starts and the other finishes. Socializing within the work time frame is limited to lunch with friends or a chat around the proverbial water cooler. Although many people have friends from work, they tend to separate their professional persona and home persona.

In China it seems to be very mixed. The first half hour of the work day is very noisy as people get their tea and water and talk about the latest news. There is a strong sense of relaxed *home life* mood. Then, all of a sudden, there is silence and work has begun. The focus is pure, and there is no breaking this while they get through their morning. Browsing the Internet or gossiping quietly about their friends is unheard of in this period. Then lunch comes along and all hell breaks loose. The office erupts with shouts and taunts and arrangements for where to eat. Small groups dash in and out until they finally disappear into little groups to eat and chat and do what they really enjoy doing, socializing over a meal. This activity of eating, talking, and being in large groups is so natural and normal in their lives that it has become an essential ritual to break the day.

When everyone comes back to the office after lunch, there is again a large community discussion with laughing and toying around. Some quickly put their heads on their desks and take a short nap. Suddenly, quiet takes over and heads are back in focus.

Home time is also a grey line. Many will leave at six for dinner and come back to finish up some work. Others will stay a little later and then go home. The younger ones will work late and then all go out together for dinner and perhaps a little Karaoke on a Friday night. Work and life seem to flow together here more than in the U.S., and the ability to mix the two makes it difficult for a Westerner to determine how we are doing on work life balance.

That being said, as people get older and children demand more time at home, this does become an issue. Husbands often work in different cities and travel each weekend or even every second weekend. Mothers may also live in the city with the child while the father stays at home in the country closer to his parents. Their willingness to live apart for years is still very difficult for me to understand.

vii Corporate Social Responsibility

There is plenty of bad press about China and its environmental challenges. There are horror stories about lead poisoning and toxic waste showing up in the drinking water of country towns. China is going through what the U.S. went through fifty years ago, but in a different way. One could argue that companies were less aware of the risks in some of their waste or actions back then, but today China has all the knowledge it needs to avoid these situations. Yet we still see them, and I am sure there are cases where the media does not get the full story. What may be surprising to know is that the educated population will not stand for this anymore. There is a strong reaction to companies putting them and their families in danger. There is not a lot they can do when the government-run companies are doing this, but for private or foreign companies, they won't tolerate it. This attitude goes all the way from pollution to the simple risk of radiation from a copier machine in the office. Child-bearing-age women will refuse to sit near the photocopier or near the IT server room for fear of radiation. Even if you bring in companies to test this, they will dispute the tests and refuse. You will always see pregnant women wearing an apron designed to reduce the radiation to their unborn child.

So running a company that focuses on these social responsibilities is important to reassure your staff that they are safe and remind them that the company takes their responsibility seriously. This can also help retain employees who are hypersensitive to areas such as this. Having a strong program will also help attract the younger candidates, as they really are concerned about their futures in China.

These are the retention drivers that need to be implemented to reduce turnovers and avail the corporation enough time to develop their people. It is important to have a stable workforce to allow the time and focus to be on growing managers and leaders rather than managing organizational stress brought on by constant turnovers, which is systemic in China right now.

IV - Solving the Creativity Gap

The 4th challenge in Chinese management is their limited creativity. If you start with the premise that creativity is stifled through the early education period, then the challenge of exposing this in the work force is difficult. The first step is to convince yourself that the ability does exist, but it is just not evident. One could argue that creativity is not learned but rather a quality you are born with. What I can attest to is that if you look for creativity in the typical business sense, then you probably won't find it. However, if you look around the city and watch closely, you will see an abundance of it.

Solving problems that eliminate the non-value-added impact to their lives is happening every day. Finding creative ways to work around laws and rules put in place by the government happens every day. The government departments are equally creative in how they react and counter these breaches. It's like the computer virus industry. For every creative anti-virus, there is an equally creative virus developed. When the government places cameras at intersections, forcing you to stop at red lights, cars will pretend to turn at the intersection, to look legal to the cameras, and then do a wide arc around the intersection to continue on straight. There really is no value to stopping at red lights and wasting time waiting, no value to yourself that is, and it's *always* about self. Building a pedestrian bridge seems like a safe idea to allow hundreds of people to cross a busy road. But this involves walking up and down steps, and that adds no value at all. So crossing the road below the bridge continues, and the new bridge becomes old and unused. So the police put up barriers in the middle of the road to stop people from getting across. Within a week the barrier has been bent and a gap is open for people to squeeze through. I agree that this isn't particularly creative, but it explains the point that where there is a problem, there will be a solution, and solutions are driven by creativity.

If we start to look for creativity in the areas of strategic thinking, the space is very empty. But put the same group in front of a practical problem that they can touch, and the juices start flowing. The team dynamic kicks in and the problem is attacked with creative vigor. The solution to generating creative thinking is to frame the goal in the form of a problem. If you are looking for a new product to market, pose this in the form of a practical problem and not a broad conceptual goal to define. Rather than ask a team to look for new innovative products out of thin air, just pose it as a problem the customer has. Out of this will come a creative solution.

Creativity for senior managers and leaders is much harder to achieve because they are not dealing with tactical problems anymore. Their world is more conceptual, with focus on areas such as future direction or organizational growth. This requires more imagination. This can be a real career-ending limitation for some, especially when they reach the level where they are competing against U.S. or European colleagues for global roles. They simply cannot compete in this area.

The good news is that with leading questioning you can get them there. These leading questions form a framework similar to a problem that tends to free the mind from having to be creative in the clouds to being creative against the challenge of a problem. So, for example, if you are looking for a manager to create a vision of what his organization should look like in three to five years, he will come up empty. It is too conceptual. However, if the request is turned into a problem, it will be tackled differently but reach the same goal. For example, ask for a detailed year-by-year growth plan that walks from where they are now to the five-year mark, building in the assumptions of growth drivers each year. This will get you there. All you need to do now is delete all the workings and details, and the three to five year picture is ready as a vision or goal.

It takes more effort to get this working, but over a period of time, serious managers will start to develop this skill themselves and will work through the steps behind the scenes. After time, this ability will improve.

V - Developing leaders

Global companies that have come to China still continue to support their operations, R&D, and support functions with expatriates. After many years, large progressive companies still cannot reach the point where senior leadership is left to the local Chinese talent. During the 2008 financial crisis, many companies took an aggressive approach to this and pulled back their expats, leaving local leadership in place. But we saw a complete reversal of this in mid-2009 when they all came back to stabilize operations. The cost of supporting expatriates in China is significant. In order to offer comparable Western housing, a car and driver, plus home-leave flights, school fees for the international schools, and tax equalizing, companies are paying $600,000 to $800,000 a year over and above their base pay. This doesn't factor in the expense of relocation and repatriation costs.

So the need to keep expatriates in China in key positions is not done for fun. It is a very serious financial consideration, and yet companies continue to do this.

Some of these roles are purely for control, and that is prudent considering the weak control culture in China. Fraud risk and potential bribing of officials is quite common in China but not acceptable to Western companies. Key leaders in these types of roles may be the norm for a while to come. However, when it comes to other senior leaders running the business units or supply chain organizations, one has to wonder why the local leaders can't fill these jobs. Local Chinese companies all have Chinese senior managers running business units and supply chain organizations, and these companies are very profitable. So where is the logic that says a Western company can't employ similar talent?

The reason is really what this book is about. It is the ability of the Chinese to compete on the global playing field under the global norms and rules. On the Chinese playing field there is no issue, but when compared to Americans and Europeans, by Americans and Europeans, there is a gap. This seems very unfair and racist on one level, and it does take extraordinary global leadership to look past this and run locally, but most cannot. If the corporation is an American company, it has such a strong American culture being pushed throughout the company via leadership and corporate policies and procedures that it is impossible to ignore, when you are trying to promote a local manager into a global role. To get support to do this, this guy has to be put in front of various American corporate executives. These executives are fly-in fly-out cultural experts, who spend two weeks a year in China and claim to be culturally unbiased. But they still compare the candidate to their U.S. counterparts. As this comparison happens, certain fundamental problems show up and are labeled as gaps in the candidate's ability.

There are ten areas that identify typical gaps in ability that the Chinese leaders need to learn if they ever want to move into roles where they are trusted and respected as a fellow American and able to run their subsidiaries in the West. One example is that Chinese leaders must not be afraid to engage in loud verbal conflicts in meetings with their international counterparts. Meetings with Spanish, Italian, or Germans can be very entertaining as the tempo gets faster and the sound gets louder. Opinions are ridiculed and ideas are defended passionately. Then they all laugh loudly at the end of the meeting and wander off to lunch together. It is not personal; its business.

But in China, it's always personal. Firstly, there is a hierarchy in each meeting that must be respected. Never contradict a superior in front of others or show him up by offering a brighter idea than his. Never fight openly or loudly because you could damage the relationship for a long time. These conflicts are best solved quietly on a one-to-one basis with careful planning that allows the other party to save face when he needs to accept your direction. The ability to allow multiple people to save face in one meeting where the conversation is so dynamic is very rare. This can only be achieved if you are senior to the rest and have command of the room. As a budding leader, the best approach, in the Chinese mind, is to be quiet and listen.

Sadly, this quiet approach is seen as a weakness by his Western counterparts. Seniors can never be considered for a leadership role by the fly-in fly-out executives if they are seen as weak. Clearly this is not fair, but if the corporation is American, then the playing field is American. The rules and culture of the field is theirs. As you step onto this field, you'd better not be playing Ping-Pong if the game is American Football.

The ten main areas that are seen as typical gaps are:

1. Broad Thinking
a. *Increase your knowledge of the company beyond China. Solutions and ideas should not be China-centric; they should be from a global perspective.*

The Chinese have fallen into the same trap as the United States, where the country is so big and diverse that there is really no reason to venture out. All the education in America is very U.S. based and is even predominately about the state you live in. If you are a Texan, then you have learned about Texas history each year at school and have seen the Alamo at least three times on school trips. The mind is trapped inside these walls, and knowledge of the geography and history of other countries is very limited. Most Americans will admit that they could not find Vietnam on a map, a country where they lost so many soldiers. The Chinese have a similar mentality when it comes to work. The focus is inside their walls, and they tend to look for solutions that work here but not in the rest of the world. They are very sheltered and don't try very hard to extend their knowledge and experience.

Developing this broader thinking of the world outside of China is fairly easy to do once you have convinced the Chinese that there is value in doing so. Some are very worldly traveled and particularly interested in U.S. politics or U.S. Pop culture. But having them extend into the other regions within their company needs some encouragement. This simple approach is through exposure to peers in other regions. Allowing them to compare processes and products across borders will give them a good reason and an opportunity to develop a cross-cultural relationship, and this relationship will drive them to become more aware of the other regions and how they think and work.

It is also important to turn this exposure into a learning opportunity. Help to emphasize the opportunity afforded them to learn about another way of operating. If nothing else, it will help to validate that their processes and methods are as good, if not better, than their counterparts.

b. Improve your ability to see past the present situation, and imagine broader impacts or advantages.

This is the issue around conceptual thinking or using imagination. More often than not the problem is solved, but the consequences to the fix are not predicted or contemplated. Often an idea is developed, but the broader impact this may have is not thoroughly assessed. Part of this limitation is driven by their selfish attitude, where someone else' problem is exactly that — *someone else' problem.* However, most of the driver is from lack of imagination. Constantly talking about wearing different hats can help force them into other people's roles and make them work through that job's impacts. This approach seems to free them from having to work through the theory of the next steps in the process. Once they are wearing that hat, they start to own it in some respects, and then the desire to improve it and make it as error free as possible kicks in. It also helps them to see the value of learning the new role, albeit theoretically.

c. Challenge the status Quo; be proactive and decisive.

I believe the problem of value add is the reason we don't see enough leaders being proactive on challenging the status quo. It also goes with the old saying, "If it ain't broke, don't fix it." Where is the value in reworking something if it seems to be working? The Western mindset in leaders is different. They often want to make their mark by reinventing the process or by at least making it look new. And, often, just this process of challenging and asking why we do things a certain way yields plenty of fruit. As you know, when the answer to the question, "Why do you do it that way?" is "Because we have always done it that way," then you are probably about to reveal a good productivity opportunity. This is an area that the Chinese leadership needs to improve on and force themselves to do. It is expected by Western leaders and one of the expectations of their playing field.

Often, to get them into the mode of reinventing it, one must convince the leaders that the process is broken. It needs to be simply forced through lean sigma khaizen events, or benchmarking, to show that the process is not at its full potential. Full potential, as described in the Six Sigma world and entitlement, is a tough sell in China. Perfection is great and important with a person's own track record of error-free processing or grades at school, but in terms of a broad process that a leader owns across many employees, this doesn't hold the same attraction. Somehow we need to be able to instill the same pride and pressure at this level as they felt as individual contributors. The leaders need to be taught that their entire group's performance, their partner's performance, and the processes they both run are a direct reflection on their own personal ability. Sounds simple, doesn't it? That's what being a manager is about. That's the basic expectation of a manager in the West, but not so obvious in the East. It comes the hard way after a failure, and you level a certain amount of criticism in front of his peer manager. This has to be done carefully, and the situation should be engineered so that he or she can still save face in the situation, but when he walks out of the room, he should still feel the failure in his gut.

Without constantly challenging the status quo, these Chinese companies will never be able to compete with their U.S. and European competitors, so it is imperative that the local managers learn how to do this as a normal way of business life.

2.Communication

a. Communication should be more concise and have more effective message mapping across all levels.

As much as the Americans love to hear themselves speak, they don't like to listen to long, drawn-out and detailed explanations from others. In Mandarin, the need to think logically also requires speech patterns to be logical as well. They don't jump over sentences, as the Americans do, when they regard them as superfluous. They need to keep the logical flow from point to point. Their American counterparts have the ability to predict a person's answer and retort before he has even opened his mouth. Skipping a step like this is disastrous for a Chinese speaker. This is still the case for Chinese with a strong command of the English language. Even with their ability to hear English and process it very quickly, their ability to respond in a skip-like motion as the Americans do is limited.

The bottom line is that it is required that these local leaders learn to get their point across quickly and in a clear way. With English being their second language, their speech is already slow and careful. This is acceptable by most, but if you compound that with a lengthy logical dialog, then they will exhaust the patience at the other end of the phone and the American side of the conversation will dominate the call.

Message mapping is also a foreign concept to the Chinese and not needed in this culture. Message mapping is designed to keep your message consistent but also help you deliver it quickly on call. In China, these messages are explained slowly, deliberately, and over many visits, so the map is not needed. However, for the U.S., this is an efficient way to communicate, and, more importantly, it is an efficient way to sell yourself and your group's achievements. When an executive walks through your area in a fly-in fly-out visit, you may only get sixty seconds with him. This message map is the only way to inform him of your value and achievements. These sixty second visits are really difficult in China considering that a relationship can take months to form. Try doing that in sixty second bites.

b. Mastering the language

Being fluent in English is important at the leadership level, as this is the language of the playing field. Europeans have the same challenge, but not all of them succeed. Language is more than just speaking, reading, and writing; it is also listening. The biggest challenge I see with Chinese who are fluent in English is that they are not able to *listen* to the question. In their haste to answer, they go with the question they thought they heard. There is nothing worse than getting an answer back to a question you never asked. This makes a really bad impression, and time-intolerant Western partners will not take the time to deal with them in the future. This can be a deal killer if done more than once, because an American cannot appreciate their challenge, especially if they are a good English speaker. Most assume that speaking and listening work in tandem. Their business partners will quickly avoid a face to face or a phone call to communicate and will resort to email (which works much better at lower levels, by the way), or they will use an intermediary to get questions answered. Once this buffer zone is created, the relationship is stunted.

3. Conflict

Be willing to engage in public conflict in order to achieve your goals.
This was talked about in the introduction, but I think it is worth noting that from what I have seen, the Chinese are very capable of direct full-contact conflict in their own environment. In their native tongue and in the comfort zone of their own culture, in a debate they will engage and raise the level of conflict to what is needed to achieve their goals. This is not a cultural limitation by any means. Unfortunately, once this same level of conflict is required in a room of Western peers, they seem to back off and play it safe. Part of this is language and the ability to express themselves in a dynamic and convincing way, but beyond this is the challenge of relationships and how they are managed in China. With other Chinese, the choice to engage an opponent in public debate to the point of embarrassing him takes place, but not often. When they choose to do so, they are very aware of what this will do to the balance, but with Western peers it is difficult to judge. Not only do the Chinese not understand how these Western opponents will react in the long term, they still see them as superior in the hierarchy simply because of their direct connection with the headquarters. Sadly, the answer is very simple because generally Westerners live in this world of direct conflict and have a great rule that is absolutely counter to the Asian way. That being: *It is business, not personal.* This term is an oxymoron in China.

4. Confidence

a. Learn to interject and speak up on conference calls and in global meetings with senior leadership.

A lot of business work in global companies is done via conference call. Video conference tools are getting better, but the time zone difference normally forces the Chinese teams to take these calls at night from home, so video equipment at the office doesn't help. Either way, there is a common agreement that you never get a question or even a whisper out of the Chinese groups on the phone. Those on the other end who have never been to or have never worked in China don't realize that there is intense concentration over here, and lots of note taking. They imagine that the room is full of a bunch of dumb-struck individuals with nothing to contribute. In reality, the phone is typically on mute and the Chinese team members are having their own side conversations to help each other catch up and come up with a consensus. They are operating as a team to reach the best understanding and response. They are also making sure the room is aligned rather than having one person from the group say something that could cause an issue with another Chinese. Their own cultural dynamic is still the controlling force in that room. I have proven this by finding much more success in this area when only one Chinese is in the room. They feel much freer to express themselves.

The American teams quickly forget that there is another party on the line and hold three conversations in the room at a speed that eliminates any easy two-way conversation. While the U.S. team is still talking and talking and talking as they love to do, the Chinese team has collected their thoughts, solved the problem, and are talking about the implementation plan. The Chinese are natural receivers and processors of information and instructions. Calls of this nature are one-sided and effective. But calls that are looking for healthy debate and discussion are a death trap for the Chinese. Not only are they often working with conceptual topics, but English is their second language and they are competing against talkative and loud Americans. Okay, not all Americans are loud, but my twelve years in Texas taught me otherwise! The real challenge for potential leaders is to command the conference call from China. Interjecting in a loud and confident voice is received very well and can be achieved with a little confidence.

b. Be more assertive and confident when presenting ideas to senior managers.

We all understand how promotions work. They are driven by senior management's *impression* of the candidate. The candidate, if promoted to senior leadership, will represent them, will reflect on them, and will impact their careers. The candidate is judged based on the same criteria that the boss is judged in his career, in his country, and in his corporate culture. One critical area where *impressions* are make-or-break is when they are touting ideas to senior leadership. What happens in this environment is that the Chinese feels that ideas are not his responsibility and that these should come from his boss. His job is to execute the ideas. But that was when he was thirty. Now that he is forty and reaching out of the execute stage and into the idea stage, he needs to start to understand that he is the guy to generate the ideas.

c. Be brave enough to challenge and contradict the manager's ideas and opinions in group meetings when needed.

As a general rule, challenging the boss is discouraged, and challenging him or her in a public meeting is unthinkable. Causing your boss to lose face in front of his peers or his subordinates is career suicide. That is true for a Chinese boss. For a Western boss, this is tolerated quite well for the most part, especially if done in a civil or diplomatic way. As you get higher in the organization and the senior leadership is older and less ego driven, this is actually encouraged. They have been around so long, they are eager to hear new ideas, and they rely on that next level to deliver the next wave that they can merely support and watch the next generation begin to take over.

To convince an Asian to challenge and debate openly like this is a momentous task. It takes a very open manager to tell them what they expect, and then when it finally happens, to not react badly but instead to commend the action. This is a two-sided challenge, where the Western half may not play fair if the challenge is sever or embarrassing. He may take advantage of the sensitivity of the Asian subordinate and strongly dominate him into submission right there. Like a scolded puppy, that will be the last time the Asian subordinate will ever challenge his superior.

d. Learn to sell yourself and get yourself exposed.

Confidence in yourself is needed in order to give your leader confidence in you. This is true in all cultures. This is normal but much more difficult when it involves self-promotion. This idea of making yourself look good in front of your boss is not accepted by the Chinese culture. People are much more sensitive to this than in the U.S. Even the slightest self-glory can be seen in a very negative light. Relationships need to be genuine and not manufactured, and so must respect. It can't be bought or sold, and it takes time. If you try to accelerate this through selling yourself or your ideas, it will not be tolerated by your peers.
The reality of this in the Western leadership world is that all of us have had to do some of this to be noticed. The world is fast-paced and attention spans are short. So when there is an opportunity — we take it. So how do we convince the Chinese to go down this road, where the fear of being ostracized by his peers is at stake? The key is to educate all the peers of this need with Western management. Turn it into a game, where they see it as fun and not as an abomination. If they understand the cross-cultural need, then they will accept it.

5. Creativity

a. Improve the ability to "Think outside the box."
This is the classic generalization about Chinese. They don't have the ability to come up with new ideas and broad concepts. This is absolutely untrue when you look around China and marvel at the amazing creativity in industry and small business. I have discussed this at length already, so suffice to say here that leading questions can help bring out this creativity in a sterile work environment surrounded by rules. Also try freeing the mind by brain storming off-site in a more creative space. Make sure these efforts are done in the local language to avoid stunting the discussion by limiting the speech.

b. Need to propose ideas for solutions to problems, not just bring the problems.
Younger employees are not expected to generate solutions to problems. They are taught to follow direction and when they encounter a problem to stop and wait. As they grow up in the organization, we start to expect solutions from them, just as we do in Western work cultures. However, there is a reluctance to do so, because it is so well taught throughout their lives that the boss provides the solutions that they have not had any practice, nor do they feel that it is their responsibility.
Splitting this into two separate problems to tackle will help drive this one home. Firstly, make sure they understand that they are expected to generate solutions at their level. This is their responsibility and they are on the hot seat to deliver. Secondly, give them some time to practice applying this, preferably earlier in their career that later, as this habit can be generated easier earlier on.

All of these challenges around the creativity discussed earlier become significantly more important for prospective leaders than they are at the junior level. Find ways to think creatively without a problem and be confident enough to bring a solution to the table that may be unconventional or risky.

6. Influencing

Develop the ability to overcome barriers introduced by interactions with other functions.

Ownership, hierarchy, and relationships are three key factors that limit the ability to influence across functions. This limitation is evident when trying to manage a task or project that requires input or change by another part of the organization. In situations where there is no reporting relationship between the two parties, there are very clear boundaries of ownership and the two peers cannot come to an agreement. The higher-level managers get involved and the hierarchy power comes into play. There is no shame in involving your boss and his boss to help resolve the conflict. This is a privilege for the boss, and he feels great value by getting involved. This works if both managers are Chinese, but if one is not, then he wonders why his subordinate cannot manage the situation himself. He is showing himself to be unable to influence others.

7. Networking

Expand your network outside of China. Expand networks vertically as well. Understand how the company politics work.

I struggled to get people to build networks outside of their comfort zones. In an environment where relationships play such a big part of society, one would think that networking would be second nature to most — and it is, but it is restricted to those with whom they work, or better said, those with whom they see as valuable to have a relationship. Networking is restricted to a one-step connection. In Linked-In terms, they would only have 1st level connections. These connections are useful, and they will develop strong relationships here. But the 2nd or 3rd level connections are not worked at because the value is not understood or predicted. The 2nd or 3rd level relationships have strategic value for Westerners and may be useful someday. We understand this on a conceptual level, and we work it. This is not the case in the East. To make it even more difficult, the 2nd level connections are often foreigners who speak a different language and are mostly senior to them. These barriers are difficult to overcome for most. My suggestion is always to stop by their office and start up a simple conversation, but there seems to be a need for a real reason or excuse to do this before they will try this approach. Cultivating relationships for the future is not understood or valued enough to invest in the uncomfortable act of starting up a casual conversation in the hallway. And even if they succeed in the first discussion, there is never any follow-through to keep the relationship warm over a period of time.

8. Organizational management

Spend more time and energy on staff development, using creative ideas and careful planning to help them reach their full potential.

In the past, staff development never required a close look. Employees were taught to leave this in the hands of their managers, and managers simply moved people as the need arose without any long-term plan in mind. As retention becomes a challenge, career planning can help to keep people in one company. This needs to become a priority. The skill set required for this is long-term strategic thinking to some extent, so a different approach is required. One approach I have found effective is to have the employee determine his ten-year goal. Then the leader has a basic problem to solve by mapping it out. They need to draw and find a realistic career path that would ensure that their employee is ready and qualified for their dream job in ten years. They are quite capable of solving this problem.

9. Stretching.

The U.S. way is constant improvement and productivity. How can we do more for less in a more accurate way? The Chinese way is: If it is working, leave it alone. One effective way to encourage this type of thinking is to add measurement. Competition between groups is fun and can drive some exciting results. Competition against another country or region will be fueled by the great strength of the People's Republic itself. They have great pride as a nation, and if you are able to tap into this, then you are well on your way to perfection.

VI Ensuring Development & Growth

Developing leaders fast enough to keep up with the compounded expansion of businesses will be key to the success of this nation. I cannot stress enough how important this is now while there is still time. Without these leaders, the progress will stall and no one will really understand why. With such fast growth, we are seeing very young talent being forced into management roles way too early. This is typically an easier way to fill these roles than to try to hire from the outside at a premium. So these poor guys get to feel the pressure at a very young age, and they are supported by equally weak and inexperienced leaders above them. Developing a lot of managers and leaders quickly and early on is the best course now.

The young talent is very eager to learn and is hungry for knowledge and experience, which makes this challenges much simpler. However, the traditional approach to development is limited to on the job training over long periods of time. Identification of high potential talent is not very structured or routine. Tagging those who have learning agility and leadership potential is fairly simple; it just needs to be done and then they need to be developed.

Those with potential will already have a track record of moving ahead of their peers. They will have curious minds and will be in the middle of everything in which they can get involved. They seem to be the go-to people when there is an issue that needs resolving quickly or when there is a complex problem that needs a team to develop a solution. They are bright, quick to understand, and they seem to be natural leaders in their world. These are the guys who you need to feed and push, as they love the excitement of the hunt and the satisfaction of success.

So how do you get them ready for the future? Push them hard while they are young. Aim to have them gain three years of experience for every two years worked. One simple approach is to rotate them between jobs quickly. Put them on a two-year rotation program where they move through three or four different positions in that time. The trick is to determine how long they should stay in each role, because each person learns at a different pace.

Step one is to make sure they are on board with the program and really want the experience. They have to surrender their immediate career goals to you and trust you as you move them through various jobs that may seem off track at times.

Once they have bought into this, you should assign them a mentor to work with them as they move along. They need to be very open and honest with their mentor to help him determine when they are ready to move on to the next job. In a typical professional role, they will take three to four months to climb the learning curve. These months are tough to handle, and the company needs to be willing to take some risk in these positions as errors will be made.

Then, just as he or she reaches the top of the learning curve and it starts to flatten out, they need to move. Your goal is to not let them get comfortable enough with the job to where they start to make improvements to the process. This will be their natural tendency. They should get to the point where they are starting to understand the process well enough that they are starting to see areas of opportunity but do not have enough time to tackle them. They are not there to add value; they are there to learn and move on. The value to the company comes later.

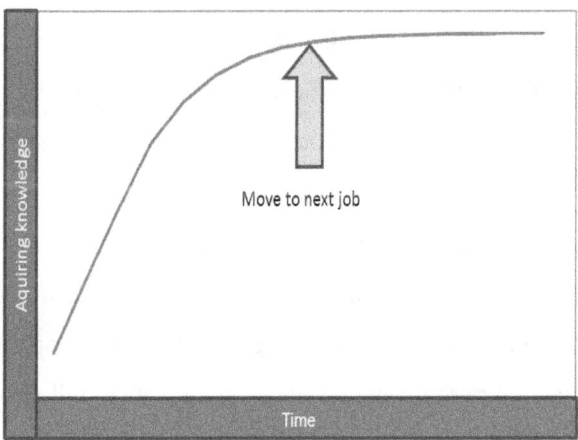

Closing

Those unfamiliar with China confuse the Communist Party with the Socialist Party. China is far from socialist, and there is no limit to how much money you can make as an individual or company here. The rules may require you to be in a position of power to succeed. Working hard at relationships with the right people in the government or having a mutually beneficial financial arrangement can help accelerate this. A lot of dinners and drinking with the right people will help decisions, construction permits, and various agreements to fall into place. Handing over red envelopes full of cash to long-term customers over Chinese New Year will ensure that the next year's sales will remain healthy. Working on lifelong relationships with people who can help when needed and vice versa is time well spent. All of these actions are normal and required on the Chinese playing field. The Chinese economy is booming, and it has only just gotten started. If I could read Mandarin, I am sure I would find a Chinese version of F. Scott Fitzgerald's *The Great Gatsby* where the plot centers around the *Chinese Dream*.

However, eventually the domestic market will be satisfied and there will be a need to reach out of China and expand their businesses in Western countries. They will need to send over their best and brightest to the U.S., to Germany, or to the UK to run these subsidiaries and compete against local companies. This competition will be on foreign turf, and the management and leaders they send over will need to know what they are doing in this foreign environment or they will be sent home with their tails between their legs.

There are significant gaps when comparing the current status of management and leaders in particular. Chinese leaders and managers need to be able to work in a world where being louder and stronger in a visual way is required in order to be respected in this world. Taking the initiative and developing the creative ideas themselves will be an important change in the way they think and operate today. Working on long-term relationships and building up trust slowly over time to compensate for the unnecessary contract will not work in this world. They cannot use little red envelopes to encourage business, nor can they find creative ways around the rule in business, or on the road, for that matter.

China is late to the global game. The game has matured and the rules have been set. Perhaps one day the referees will be Chinese, but right now they will have to learn how to play under the current rules if they want to reach their full potential.

The good news for China is that there are so many amazing qualities already in place within their world. Their positive attitude, their teamwork, and their ability to learn so quickly have put them in good stead. Wrap that in the motivation to be excellent at everything they do and you have an impressive beginning. Now, put this package behind their huge population, who all have a deep yearning to grow and be wealthy, and the chances of success are clear.

If all the members of the U.S. Congress and Senate were able to see and appreciate this potential in China, we would see bi-partisan government action like we haven't seen since 9/11/2001. They would make economic policy decisions to move the U.S. quickly out of this deadlock that we have been in for so many years. If the U.S. is to remain the superpower they like to be known as, then they should pay heed to what is hidden behind that Great Wall.

www.ingramcontent.com/pod-product-compliance
Lightning Source LLC
Chambersburg PA
CBHW051542170526
45165CB00002B/837